HOW TO BUILD AND FLY
ELECTRIC MODEL AIRCRAFT

HOW TO BUILD AND FLY
ELECTRIC MODEL AIRCRAFT

ROBERT SCHLEICHER

WITH SPECIAL THANKS TO JAMES R. BARR

MBI

First published in 2005 by MBI, an imprint of
MBI Publishing Company, Galtier Plaza, Suite 200,
380 Jackson Street, St. Paul, MN 55101-3885 USA

The information in this book is true and complete
to the best of our knowledge. All recommendations
are made without any guarantee on the part of the
author or Publisher, who also disclaim any liability
incurred in connection with the use of this data or
specific details.

This publication has been prepared solely by MBI
Publishing Company and is not approved or
licensed by any other entity. We recognize that some
words, model names, and designations mentioned
herein are the property of the trademark holder. We
use them for identification purposes only. This is
not an official publication.

MBI titles are also available at discounts in bulk
quantity for industrial or sales-promotional use.
For details write to Special Sales Manager at MBI
Publishing Company, Galtier Plaza, Suite 200,
380 Jackson Street, St. Paul, MN 55101-3885 USA.

ISBN-13: 978-0-7603-2139-3
ISBN-10: 0-7603-2139-6

Editor: Amy Glaser
Design: Russell Kuepper

Printed in China

On the frontispiece: The best place to learn how
take off from the ground is to find a stretch of
pavement or sidewalk so the model won't bounce or
pitch unpredictably.

On the title page: Josh Glavin attached some
1/16-inch carbon fiber rods to bottom of the wings
of his E-Flite Ultimate to improve the model's
stability and crash resistance.

On the back cover 1: Jorge Castorena has
maneuvered his E-Flite Ultimate from a hovering
position and the aircraft now is about a fourth
of the way through a tight full 360 degree knife
edge loop.

On the back cover 2: The Hobbico (from Great
Planes' Electrifly line) Triton will charge Li-Poly and
NiCd or NiMH batteries. *Copyright Hobbico, Inc.,
used with permission*

Table of Contents

CHAPTER 1
Flying Freedom

SOAR LIKE THE WIND. Fly like an eagle. These are just two of the many allusions of the yearning we have to be free of the force of gravity. Flying is freedom. The next best thing is controlling our very own flying machine. If that control can be just a step away from controlling the flight with our mind, we are that much closer to freedom.

Alan Boyington's GWS Slow Stick has its ailerons set for a banked turn under full control and over 50 yards from his radio control transmitter.

FREEDOM
Apply the concept of freedom to a model airplane and the dream would be to control the airplane with our minds—to make that aircraft turn and bank and loop and hover and sail at will. Electric-powered model aircraft make that dream possible.

Rubber bands supplied power for the early model airplanes, and there is still a hobby of rubber-band powered flight. The rubber bands are silent and harmless enough that the models can be flown indoors or out. The search for more power and longer flight duration led to the use of fuel-burning engines, but these powerplants were noisy and the general public considered them dangerous (mostly because of the noise). A few decades ago fliers began experimenting with electric motors, but performance and flight duration were always severely limited by the excessive weight of the battery. Today, the lithium-polymer battery and efficient brushless motors have made it possible to fly almost as long and as well with electric power as with fuel. Now we fliers are back to the days of silent flight, of being able to fly in a backyard or in a park or indoors.

TECHNOLOGY

The mechanics of powered model flight have finally caught up with our dreams for flying model airplanes. Technology has changed the hobby of flying model airplanes. Today, you can choose between fuel and battery power and have nearly identical performance from the model aircraft. You can fly identical model airplanes through identical maneuvers for nearly the same amount of time with an electric-powered model as you can a fuel-powered model. The combined weight of the electric motor and batteries needed for a 30-minute flight is very close to weight of the engine, fuel tank, and fuel. The amount of energy that is required to keep a model aircraft flying can be achieved with either electricity or fuel.

Model airplane hobbyists refer to the internal combustion engines used in model aircraft as "fuel" or "glow" engines. Some of the giant scale aircraft use small four-stroke engines, but the majority of model aircraft use two-stroke engines with no valves. These motors burn special fuels with higher octane ratings than common gasoline, and the lubrication is mixed in with the fuel. The term "glow" applies to the spark plug that ignites the fuel. In two-stroke model airplane engines the spark plug is hot at all times, so it literally glows. I'll refer to all of these engines as fuel-burning powerplants.

ELECTRIC POWER

Until recently, the weight of the container for the electricity (battery) was much greater than the weight of the fuel (and fuel tank) when both delivered the same amount of energy. The search for lighter batteries to power everything from cell phones to automobiles to space ships continues. Technology has produced the lithium-polymer (Li-Poly) battery, which has been a major breakthrough in electric-powered flight for model airplanes. Batteries are likely to get even lighter as technology develops. Right now, the Li-Poly battery is powerful and light enough to be a pound-for-pound replacement of fuel as an energy source needed for model aircraft power. You can still fly a bit longer or power a somewhat larger airplane with fuel than with electricity, but do you really care if you can only

Jorge Castorena flies his Extra 3-D foam ARF into the beginning of an aerobatic loop.

fly 30 minutes on a battery charge as opposed to 45 minutes on a tank of fuel?

Those searching for more power and/or longer duration flying times have discovered that brushless electric motors are many times more efficient than traditional brush-style motors. The brushless motors were expensive, but the demand in industry has become so great that the costs have tumbled and brushless motors now power a large proportion of electric model aircraft. The efficient brushless electric motors require far less electrical energy. Combine that motor with ultra-lightweight Li-Poly batteries and the electric-powered model aircraft will fly with the best of the fuel-power aircraft.

EFFICIENT PRODUCTION

Technology has changed the hobby of flying model aircraft in many ways beyond supplying lightweight and silent power. Modern materials like carbon fiber have been incorporated into model aircraft construction to produce models that are many times stronger and lighter. Both extruded and expanded polyfoam have been developed to make it relatively easy to manufacture complex shapes with minimal weight. And modern model aircraft designs often combine modern materials with traditional construction methods. For example, a stick model covered with tissue can be extremely rugged if the wing tips and a few other areas are reinforced with strips of carbon fiber. Some of the more advanced competition fliers have wings and fuselages formed from carbon fiber. Looking back into the history of model aircraft, the classic tissue-covered models with balsa framework are great airframes for electric power.

Many of the flying model aircraft, especially the almost-ready-to-fly (ARF) models, are now produced in China. Chinese production has considerably reduced the cost of the high-performance electric-powered models. You can buy an ARF airplane complete with motor, batteries, and radio control transmitter for less than $300, or a plane capable of winning a flying contest for less than $400. There are even ARF models made with traditional balsa structures and polymer covering that cost less than $100.

The motor, battery pack, ESC, and servos are all visible on the ultra-lightweight GWS Slow Stick.

Chris Hume hand-launches his GWS Slow Stick.

THE FLIGHT DECK

If it flies in the real world, you can buy or build it as a model with electric power. In fact, just about anything is available as an ARF model. The foamy models, cut from sheets of expanded polyfoam, are the least expensive models and most are surprisingly strong, thanks to strategically placed carbon fiber reinforcing rods. Some of them even have three-dimensional (3-D) fuselages. The choices of molded-polyfoam airplanes include near-exact scale replicas of real airplanes like the P51D Mustang, as well as aircraft designed to take maximum advantage of the wing sizes and shapes developed expressly for model airplanes. The fuselage and wings of some models are vacuum-formed plastic to produce light, but nearly indestructible, replicas of real aircraft as well as designed-as-a-model aircraft. There's even a wide choice of twin- and four-motored electric-powered aircraft. Sailplanes with fold-back propellers and ducted fan jet aircraft models are available from several firms. The choice of helicopters range from machines no larger than this book that can be flown indoors, to massive three-foot-long choppers. For the light-hearted, there are electric-powered ornithopters, which are machines that flap their wings to fly like a radio-controlled bird.

BUILDERS OR FLIERS

The hobby of flying model aircraft encompasses both builders and fliers. Today, the best-selling model aircraft by a factor of about 10 is the ARF plane. Usually ARF means you slip the wings in place, snap the rubber bands around the battery, and plug in the receivers, the electronic speed control (ESC), and motor.

There are thousands of kits available for those who want to build their own models. Hobby magazines feature plans to build your own flying aircraft

Frank Dilatusch flies his
Czech Alpha ARF replica
of the P-51D Mustang.

The Czech Alpha P-51D Mustang is
a painted Styrofoam ARF model.
GWS offers a similar ARF model.

Tim Goldstein's highly modified Piccolo Pro helicopter.

models that are designed to be powered by electric motors. The relatively light and balanced weight of the electric motor and batteries, compared with the more concentrated mass of an engine and fuel tank, somewhat reduce the potential damage from crashes, so it is more attractive to invest the hours to build your own.

THE SCIENCE OF FLIGHT

Flight is not quite as complex as rocket science. In fact, the physics of flight are simple enough to allow modelers to experiment to produce better performance from their model aircraft. Most of us will settle for the aerodynamics that the model manufacturer provides, so the shape of the aircraft can be a given. If you prefer to design and build your model aircraft, by all means do so. What we can control and modify is the efficiency of the power that propels the aircraft.

Performance efficiency is based on the weight, the available electrical energy, and the ability of the propeller to make maximum use of that energy. One

of the challenges of electric-powered aircraft is to match the motor to the batteries to the propeller to provide the maximum performance for that model.

Fliers have devised computer programs like ElectriCalc and MotoCalc to combine the variables of the available electric power from the batteries, the needs of the motor and propeller, and—in some cases—the choice of gear-reduction between motor and propeller. You can program the ESC so that the motor gets the most efficient flow of power from the battery. The programs can also help you determine if the motor would be more efficient with a gearbox. The propeller diameter and pitch can be selected to match certain conditions. The propeller may need to be changed to provide the best thrust from the most efficient combination of batteries, motor, motor speed, and propeller speed, diameter, and pitch. Even seemingly minor variables like humidity or a change in wind velocity may also be balanced with a change in propeller pitch. There's more information on achieving maximum performance in Chapter 8.

THINK IT AND IT HAPPENS

The simplest form of control for a model airplane is to let the thing fly itself. Aircraft modelers call it free flight. It works surprisingly well if you learn the skills of balancing the model, setting the trim just right, and perfecting the launch. There is a special appeal to flying a model that flies by itself. You can do it with rubber bands, fuel-burning engines, or electric motors.

To get up close and personal with a model, modelers devised the tethered or U-control flight. Two wires are used to move the elevators up or down to allow the plane to climb or dive. With a roaring motor 50 feet away at the end of the two-wire tether, you do get a feeling of being in the aircraft. Skilled fliers can perform most aerobatic maneuvers with a U-control plane. Some folks have substituted electric motors for a fuel-burning engine. The planes fly just as well.

Radio control allowed fliers to go beyond the set controls of free-flight and tethered U-control, and to send their thoughts of movement through the air at the flick of their fingertips. With practice, flying a model airplane by radio control becomes an exercise of the mind—you really forget what your fingers are doing, much as you forget what your hands and feet are doing when driving an automobile.

ADVANCED AEROBATICS

You can make your aircraft fly at your very thought. It can literally land gently in your hand, swoop to a three-point runway landing, or with a float plane, glide to a water landing. The model can be flown so far away that you can barely see it or brought within a few feet of you. The model can dive like a falcon, soar like a hawk, hover like a hummingbird, or glide with grace of a gull. Allusions to birds are almost unavoidable because a well-practiced pilot really

This HalAir MiG-29 has a ducted fan that is powered by an electric motor.

Steven Stratt built from scratch this replica of the Fokker D.VIII, which flew in World War I. He built the model with a fuel-burning engine, but converted it to electric.

A group of fliers at the Northeast Electric Aircraft Technology (NEAT) national meet in New York admire a Cactus Aviation Extra on the flight line.

Electric-powered delta-wing aircraft are great learning fliers.

Radio-control ornithopters simulate the wing-flapping flight of birds.

does appear to command the aircraft as he or she might with a trained bird.

Recent advances in radio control transmitters and ever-more responsive servo motors have made it possible to control a model airplane or helicopter as well as you might control the real version. In fact, fliers discovered that they can perform aerobatic maneuvers that are all but impossible with real aircraft. Model helicopters can fly upside down; model airplanes can perform stunts while flying sideways (knife-edge maneuvers) and more. Conventional aerobatic stunts like barrel rolls and loops are simple. Model fliers can go further and make their airplane models hover by hanging on the prop like a helicopter. There is now more than enough power available with an electric-powered aircraft to do any stunt that's possible with fuel-powered aircraft.

FLY 'EM (ALMOST) ANYWHERE

The fuel-burning engine for a model aircraft has always presented a problem. For starters, the engine is literally exploding a 100 times a second—and it sounds and feels like it. The noise and the power that noise implies have made model airplanes the scourge of many communities. Fliers have been forced to find flying fields far removed from civilization to avoid possible accidents with those miniature flying machines.

Since it is no longer necessary to have a whining fuel-powered motor, your choices of places to fly have expanded. Freedom from fuel means that you can fly almost anywhere, even in your backyard. There are dozens of airplanes and helicopters small enough that you can fly them in your living room, and many flying meets are conducted inside gymnasiums. Most cities and towns have regulated the flights of model aircraft to specific flying fields far away from the general population, but fliers of electric-powered aircraft often find much more convenient flying fields. Your local hobby dealer can probably tell you where the local fliers meet on the weekends. There is of course, the danger of an errant aircraft hitting someone, but the impetus for those distant fields has been noise. You still need a landowner's permission to use his or her property for anything, including flying. You certainly don't want to endanger anyone, so don't even consider flying in populated parks. Silent flight, however, is far more acceptable to non-fliers. You can fly many of these machines in empty parks.

On any sunny Sunday, you'll likely find a host of pilots at a local flying field, like the Rocky Mountain E-Flyers in Arvada, Colorado.

CHAPTER 2
Simple Electric Aircraft

ELECTRIC POWER has re-created the hobby of flying model aircraft. You no longer need the skills of a miniature cabinetmaker or the reflexes of a billiards pro to fly model aircraft. You can get started with a $100 ready-to-fly model that includes everything except a battery charger. Or you can buy an ARF micro model and fly it in your living room, where you can learn what it takes to master the fundamentals of flight. Then you can later apply those skills to the flights of massive four-engine aircraft or aerobatic helicopters. There are virtually no limits on what you can fly. It's entirely your choice how much time and energy you want to spend to achieve the ultimate in powered flight.

Jorge Castorena's Northeast Sailplanes' Extra 3-D has been upgraded with a Rotex 2/6/15 motor and Li-Poly battery pack.

YOUR FIRST ELECTRIC-POWERED AIRCRAFT
Find out which aircraft are best for beginners in your area by talking to people at your local hobby shop. Also try to locate the nearest flying site and the times the fliers meet and visit the site on a flying day. Often, the best model for a beginner is an aircraft that is readily available locally and one that several of the fliers have purchased and flown successfully. What's the most popular beginner aircraft in one area may not be the most popular model in another area.

Better aircraft models are introduced quite frequently, so last year's choice might not be this year's choice, which is why I hesitate to recommend any particular model, transmitter, motor, or battery. I'll tell you what experienced flyers were using when I prepared this book, and you can update this information with the local fliers, hobby dealers, and the newest magazine articles. Today, the same people may be using something completely different. Frankly, constantly searching for the best can be frustrating, and to a large degree pointless, because all of the most exciting aircraft are incredibly easy to fly.

A GWS Slow Stick soars over the Rockies.

The HobbyZone
Slow V is a simple
ARF model that is
available with a three-
channel transmitter.

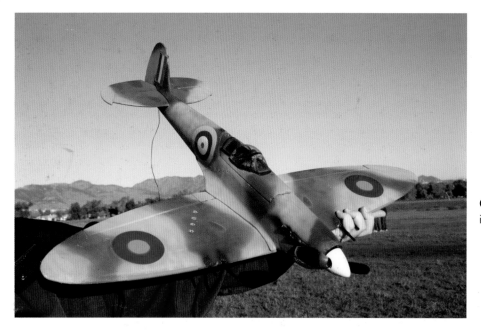

Chuck Shafer's GWS Spitfire is an ARF foam model.

Frank Dilatush's Kyosho Spree is an ARF model with conventional stick model construction.

18

READY-TO-FLY PACKAGES

Your hobby dealer can offer a wide range of complete turn-key packages to get you started by flying electric-powered radio control aircraft. The packages include the motor with a matched propeller, ESC, and battery pack to take all the guesswork out of selecting components. Some package deals even include the receiver and transmitter, but most don't and you will need them. I would suggest that you buy the best transmitter you can afford, preferably one with four or more channels and adjustable radio frequencies as described later in this chapter.

ARF AIRCRAFT

ARF is short for "almost ready to fly." These aircraft packages are not really kits, but they require 1 to 5 hours of assembly time. The wings, fuselage, rudder, and stabilizer are usually assembled, but one or more may need to be attached to the model. Also, the servo motors may need installed and adjusted, and the motor will need to be fitted. The better ARF aircraft include all the hardware you will need, but you may have to purchase the servo motors, receiver, and ESC.

I would suggest you consider purchasing either a ready-to-fly or an ARF package so you know you will have a model that is designed to fly from the first launch. Later, if you wish, you can upgrade the power and battery pack.

HOW BIG?

The electric-powered model airplanes are commonly divided into five categories, based essentially on the size of the model. Obviously, the larger models will require more power, and with more power, there's more potential for speed.

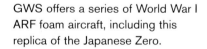

Several firms offer ARF foam versions of the F4U Corsair gull wing World War II fighter, including Hobby Lobby and this GWS model.

GWS offers a series of World War I ARF foam aircraft, including this replica of the Japanese Zero.

PARKING LOT, PARK FLYERS, AND BACKYARD FLYERS

Most of the model aircraft you'll see in this book fall into the parking lot, park flyers, and backyard flyers category for one reason: These are by far the most popular models because they are the easiest aircraft to fly, and size-for-size, the least expensive. Some of these models are a bit too large to be flown indoors, but they are sturdy enough to be flown in mild winds. These are the models that have fueled the explosive growth of flying model aircraft over the past few years.

Typically, a parking lot, park flyer, or backyard flyer aircraft will weigh between 8 and 14 ounces. Some of the model importers have coined similar names, like Horizon's Park Zone and HobbyZone models, Hobbico's Fly Zone, Great Planes' Electrify Park Flyers, Ikarus' Shock Flyer, and others. These are the medium-size models. You would be wise to choose your first radio control aircraft from the models in this size range because they are all designed for entry-level fliers. The better models in this range can be upgraded with larger motors and battery packs.

The magic of molded Styrofoam has allowed the manufacturers to produce low-cost, easy-to-fly ARF models of real aircraft, like this Tiger Moth biplane from GWS.

This Piper Cub is an ARF park flyer from Hobbico and has a wooden framework with a polyurethane covering. The motor has a gear-drive propeller. Copyright Hobbico, Inc., used with permission.

Chuck Shafer's DeHavilland Beaver is an ARF foam model from GWS that he upgraded with a brushless motor and external battery pack.

The SIG Rascal is an ARF model with pre-assembled
stick wings, fuselage, rudder, and elevator.

Dave Hock's GWS-brand Estarter is one
of the easy-to-fly aircraft that can perform
aerobatics and is small enough to be
flown indoors.

ULTRA MICRO AIRCRAFT

Now that you know which size aircraft are the most popular, I'll cover the remaining four sizes. The smallest electric-powered aircraft are in the Ultra Micro class, which weigh less than two ounces with batteries. Ultra Micro aircraft can be small enough to fit in the palm of your hand. Typically, an Ultra Micro airplane has a 15-inch wingspan, a 3- to 5-inch propeller, a 3-channel receiver, and can carry 120-milliamp-hour (mAh) nickel metal hydride (NiMH) batteries. These models are intended only for flying indoors and are essentially the refuge for modelers who prefer to build from scratch.

SUB MICRO AIRCRAFT

The Sub Micro aircraft models are a bit more practical than the Ultra Micro models, but they are still a bit challenging for a beginner. A Sub Micro airplane usually weighs between 2 and 3 ounces. Kits and some ARF models are now available in the Sub Micro class.

Z-Planes also has a series of slightly smaller Word War II aircraft with larger wings, rudder, and stabilizer for better indoor flying. Dynamics Unlimited has a foam version of the P-38 with a full fuselage and a 19-inch wingspan. The single-motor models weigh just under 3 ounces with motor, receiver, servos, and a 120-mAh NiMH battery pack.

D J Aerotech offers a series of World War II–era profile models, including a Folke Wulfe Bf109; F4U Corsair; P-51 Mustang, Zero and Spitfire; and even a twin-motored P-38 Lightning. Some of the tiny cut-foam aircraft, such as the Wattage Micro Flyer or the Aero-X from Estes also fall in the Sub Micro category.

The *Spirit of St. Louis* is an ARF model from Electifly by Hobbico. It has a foam fuselage and wings with a gear-drive motor. Copyright Hobbico, Inc., used with permission.

MICRO AIRCRAFT

The Micro aircraft models weigh between 3 and 8 ounces. These are the most popular aircraft for indoor flight and they can be flown outdoors on very calm days. There are a number of small foam aircraft—including some of the GWS and Radio Shack models—that fit in the Micro category.

Some of the trainer aircraft, like the GWS Slowstick, are light enough to qualify as Micro aircraft but powerful enough to be flown outdoors. These models are designed to be powered by a motor with 280 to 300 power levels and typically 270-mAh battery packs.

SPEED 400 AIRCRAFT

The largest and most powerful electric-powered aircraft fall in the Speed 400 category. The number 400 is the arbitrary measure of the motor's power, but there are no specific rules for motor performance. The 380 and 400 motors are currently the largest in common use. The Speed 400 models are exclusively intended for flying outdoors. The models range widely in size and power, from re-motored park flyers to four-motored aircraft with 6-foot wingspans. Typically, a battery pack with between 800 and 1100 mAh will be needed.

The Parkzone Slo-V can be flown slow enough to be used indoors or out.

There are dozens of ARF electric-powered sailplanes. Ron Evans built this Glassair from a HalAir kit.

The Siren electric-powered (with a folding propeller) ARF sailplane from ElectriFly has a carbon fiber fuselage and carbon fiber reinforced wings with a 79-inch wingspan. Copyright Hobbico, Inc., used with permission.

The E-Flite Tribute is a profile airplane with full 3-D flight capability.

Profile models sometimes portray just a rough outline of the aircraft's shape, but their extremely light weight makes them excellent fliers with little chance of damage if crashed.

PROFILE MODEL AIRCRAFT

The model manufacturers offer dozens of relatively inexpensive ARF models that are simple, flat pieces of die-cut or laser-cut foam or balsa. Some of these models have the shape or profile of a popular real aircraft, like a P-51 Mustang. Gamma Star Models even offers a profile model of the P-38 Lightning with a 40-inch wingspan. Many of the profile models are special model aircraft designs with engineered and tested shapes to fly as well as the best full-fuselage models. There are also many models that have a profile fuselage with airfoil wings, but a flat rudder and stabilizer.

The profile planes that are designed for aerobatics or even 3-D flight are often a wise choice for a beginner because they are so lightweight that little damage is done when they do crash. And with simple foam sheet construction, repairs can usually be made quickly with foam-safe cyanoacrylate cement (CA), a hot glue gun, or strapping tape. The profile models are an extremely good value because they offer maximum flying performance at the absolute minimum cost. The larger profile models are often reinforced with strip of carbon fiber (a modification you can make as well), which runs near the wing-mount in the fuselage from the motor mount to the tail and near the leading edge of the wing from wing tip to wing tip.

Frank Dilatusch upgraded his Northeast Sailplane 2Cool so it is capable of full aerobatic flight, as shown in Chapter 8.

PICK YOUR FAVORITE

The five different sizes of aircraft—and whether the models have a profile fuselage and wings or are full shapes—merely provide the broad categories. Within each of these are different types of models, from exact scale to powered sailplanes to 3-D or aerobatic model aircraft. If your hobby dealer or club does not have recommendations for your first or second electric-powered radio control aircraft, consider some of the ones listed here.

There are a few trainer aircraft models that seem to fly more easily, crash less frequently, and yet provide the response to controls that experienced model aircraft flyers expect. The list changes weekly as newer and better models are introduced. The GWS Slow Stick is an ungainly looking model reminiscent of a low-wing World War I Fokker. The wings are struts with a top fabric covering and the fuselage is an aluminum stick. Its simple construction and light weight (it's really built as much like a kite as an airplane) make it extremely stable but still responsive to transmitter input. It is also one of the better crash survivors. The model can be upgraded by replacing the brushed motor with a brushless motor like the Himaxx 5400. Similar aircraft (and upgrades) like the Parkzone Slo-V and Wattage Lite Stik, and some from several other makers, are available.

The solid foam models are excellent airframes for electric power. The GWS and Northeast Sailplane series of World War II aircraft, which includes a P-51 Mustang, F4U Corsair, and Focke Wulfe Bf109, fly well and are stable enough to perform with much more powerful motor and battery packs.

The foam-construction 3-D aerobatic models, like the Ikarus Shock-Flyer and E-Flite Tribute, are the least expensive models to use when learning to fly aerobatics and 3-D maneuvers. Cermark's Banchee, Kyosho's Spree, Esprit's Sukkol, Hanger 9's Twist, Hobby Lobby's Hell Raiser, and Northeast's Mamba are just a few of the aircraft that have pre-assembled stick structure wings, rudder and stabilizer, and are capable of advanced aerobatics and 3-D flight.

POWERED SAILPLANES

You also have a wide choice of powered sailplanes, from the Carl Goldberg Electra or Great Planes' Ventura entry-level series to the 2-meter wingspan giants with fiberglass fuselages like Kyosho's Ciero 2000G or Esprit's Pulsar. The powered sailplanes have folding propellers to lessen the drag when the aircraft is soaring. Most of the models can be restarted mid-flight to gain more altitude. An experienced flyer can keep an electric-powered sailplane in the air for 4 hours and more because it only needs to occasionally use battery power for moving the control surfaces.

The Hobby Lobby Hell Raiser profile biplane flies into a rainstorm at the 2004 NEAT meet in New York.

MULTI-MOTORED MODEL AIRCRAFT

There are several choices of ARF multi-engined model aircraft that range in size—from the tiny Z-Planes P-38 Lightning to the micro-size Aerotech P-38 Lightning, and from the Mountain Model and Hobby Lobby's versions with 38-inch wingspans to the Kondor Models Giant Scale P-38. Dynamics Unlimited has a foam version of the P-38. Polk's, Great Plane's ElectriFly and GWS offer twin-engined replicas of the DC-3 or Douglas C-47 with a 72-inch wingspan, and Hobbico has a replica of twin-engined C-160 with a 72-inch wingspan. Cedar Hobbies has the high-wing Airbus and a four-motored B-29 with a compact 40-inch wingspan, and GWS has a four-motored C-130 Cargotrans high-winged model with a 44-inch wingspan. These models include instructions for wiring multiple motors with the appropriate ESC for each motor.

This DC-3 is an ARF model with a fiberglass fuselage and factory assembled, plastic-covered, wood-braced wings. The Electrifly model from Hobbico has a 59-inch wingspan. Copyright Hobbico, Inc., used with permission.

Electric power makes it relatively simple to have multi-engined aircraft. This GWS replica of the C-47 is an ARF foam model.

29

The Slinger ARF from ElectriFly has a pusher propeller and a 49-inch wingspan. Copyright Hobbico, Inc., used with permission.

There are dozens of delta-wing foam models that look like jets, but are powered by rear-mounted electric motors and propellers like this HobbyZone F-27 Stryker. Newer versions have USAF camouflage paint and markings and built-in combat capability, as described in Chapter 8.

JET PLANES

There are dozens of replicas of conventional and delta wing jet fighters, but most have a conventional propeller mounted at the rear. Just because it looks like a jet doesn't mean it will fly like one. A true jet has a fuel-burning engine. Still, the models with jet aircraft shapes can be incredibly quick, with speeds that are proportional to real jets.

Parkzone has an F-27 Stryker delta-winged model that looks and flies like a jet. The F-27 Stryker has a single direct-drive 480 motor and a 37-inch wingspan. It's available ready-to-fly, includes the transmitter and installed receiver, and is fully aerobatic.

DUCTED FAN JETS

Model airplane builders have adapted the ducted fan powerplant to produce much of the speed and the sound of a true jet. The first ducted fan engines were powered by conventional fuel-burning model aircraft engines. Today, there is a full range of ducted fan motors available that are designed to be powered by electric motors. A true ducted fan powerplant is a cylinder about 4 to 6 inches in diameter and the fan blades are inside the cylinder. The ducted fan operates much like a turbine, with a special propeller (usually with five blades designed like a fan rather than a two-, three-, or four-bladed propeller) enclosed inside the cylinder. Electric-powered ducted fan engines have much the same sound as a jet and produce a similar performance. The fan blades can turn at over 22,000 rpm. There are several ARF ducted fan models including GWS' B2 bomber and A10, Kyosho's FV-1000, Hal Air's MiG-29, and Hobby Lobby's MiG-15 models. Ducted fan powerplants with electric motors are available from Hobby Lobby, GWS, and other suppliers.

The ducted fan powerplant looks, sounds, and performs like a real jet engine. The GWS model of the A10 Attack aircraft has two ducted fan motors.

This is a HalAir MiG-29 is a balsa wood kit aircraft built by Chris True and fitted with a GWS ducted fan powerplant.

FLY THE BIRDS' WAY

You also have the option of flying a radio control electric-powered aircraft that really does fly like a bird. These machines are called ornithopters and they fly by flapping their wings. Ornithopter Zone, Kinkade Ornithopters, and others offer several sizes of these motorized birds.

There are also some cloth-covered flying wings, like the Ace Sim RC Carbon Falcon, that can soar. The wings do not move on these aircraft, but the fabric and framework re-create the lift of a kite or a bird's set wings so the models appear to glide like birds.

GIANT SCALE MODELS

The giant scale models you covet are now available at incredibly low prices as the ARF models built in China. Polk's Fokker DR-1 Tri-Plane has a 40-inch wingspan and is hand-built, but it can be assembled in less than an hour. The model is constructed with a stick-and-polymer covering like a traditional handmade model. This one, though, is ready-to-fly after you've attached the wings, stabilizer, and fuselage, and added the motor and control gear of your choice. The model is designed for a four-channel radio and a geared Speed 400 motor.

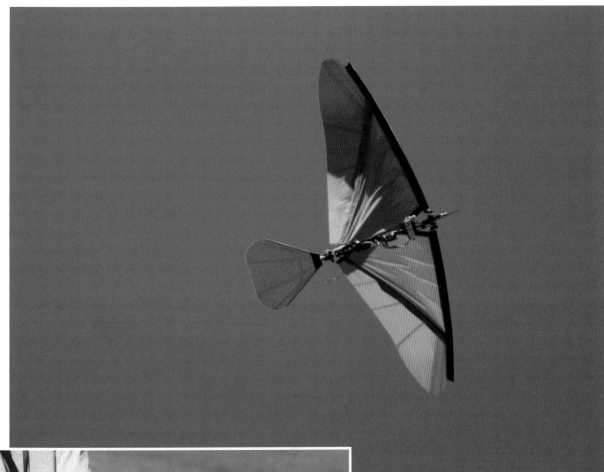

The ornithopters link the electric motor to levers that move the model's wings so it literally flies like a bird.

The small delta-wing aircraft, like the Ace Sim RC Carbon Falcon, can be flown indoors or outdoors.

Kondor Models has a full range of giant scale models. The largest is the twin-motored P-38 Lightning with an 86-inch wingspan, fiberglass fuselages, and balsa-covered foam wings. The P-38 can weigh as much as 15 pounds—this is the opposite end of the size spectrum from Dynamic Unlimited's P-38 with its 19-inch wingspan.

FULL INSTRUMENT READ-OUTS

Eagle Tree Productions offers a Seagull Wireless Dashboard flight data acquisition device. A featherweight transmitter is mounted to the surface of the model. The Seagull includes a digital dashboard that you can mount near your transmitter. The Seagull dashboard system provides up to 20 channels of data. With the Seagull you can see critical data parameters in real-time on the liquid crystal display (LCD), and set audible alarms for speed, voltage, engine temperature, rpm, cumulative mAh, and much more. The Seagull displays positions of up to four servo motors (with settable user-friendly names on the LCD), the receiver's battery voltage, the speed of the model with each sample, the flight's altitude and climb rate with each sample, the rpm of the model's motor, and up to two channels of temperature. Optional expanders for measuring G-force, electric motor current/voltage, and other parameters are available from Eagle Tree Systems. Seagull Wireless Dashboard with flight data acquisition kit is $370.

Kondor Model's twin-motored P-38 Lightning has an 86-inch wingspan with a fiberglass fuselage and balsa-covered foam wings.

There are a number of stick kits with balsa inner structures and polyester covering that are designed for easy conversion from fuel or rubber-band power to electric power for flying indoors or outdoors.

RCAT Systems is a supplier of wireless data acquisition solutions and electronics products for both full-size aircraft and for models. The RCATS Sport Unit (RCATS0900S or RCATS2400S) 900-megahertz and 2.4-gigahertz versions will provide in-flight information on your laptop computer screen. The RCATS kit includes the data collection unit (DCU); transmitter; receiver; rpm sensor and magnet; virtual instrument panel software; manual on/off slide switch; 7-inch brass pitot/static probe; hookup tubing; T-fitting and two quick disconnects; two standard thermocouples; receiver voltage measurement adapter; mounting Velcro; virtual instrument panel software; and a detailed instruction manual. The fixed wire transmitter antenna version is included. The unit weighs about 6 ounces and sells for $720.

ELECTRIC VERSUS FUEL POWER

If you have fuel-powered aircraft, you can actually measure the difference in performance between fuel- and electric-powered aircraft. The Seagull's products' data allows you to record the performance of either fuel- or electric-powered aircraft. Several modelers have attached Seagull units to nearly identical aircraft. The read-outs on those units' screen and actual in-flight performance suggest that the more powerful brushless electric motors (such as the AXI 4120) provide performance nearly equal to the 0.9-ci displacement fuel engines. Flight times are governed by the size of the fuel tank, fuel consumption, or the size of the battery pack. A 6800-mAh Li-Poly battery pack will usually fly aerobatic maneuvers for about 30 minutes.

Most of the major manufacturers offer at least one ARF model with optional floats for takeoffs and landings on water. This is the GWS Tiger Moth with GWS 535 floats installed.

FLYING FROM THE WATER

Some manufacturers offer the option of floats for some of their ready-to-fly and ARF models. The floats allow you to re-create the performance of real aircraft taking off from the water and landing on the water. They can also be used on thick and soft grass. The floats do not affect the aircraft's performance as much as their bulk and weight might suggest, because most are designed with a built-in airfoil to at least lift their own weight during flight. It is not recommended, however, that you attempt much aerobatics because the floats upset the potential aerobatic performance of the model. GWS offers a number 535 float kit that can be adapted to most of the medium-size park flyer airplanes.

ATTENTION-GETTING STROBES

If you want to attract some attention at the flying field, consider fitting your model with operating strobe lights on the wingtips and tail. High-intensity light-emitting diodes (LED) require minimal power and produce light bright enough grab your attention. Curtek Lighting and others offer special pre-wired landing light kits that are simple to install.

Curtek Lighting and others offer special pre-wired warning light kits that are easy to install.

CHAPTER 3
The Mechanics of Model Flight

THE ONLY SOUND you hear when these electric aircraft perform is the air screw (propeller) slicing and beating its way through the air and, if the aircraft is close enough, the whoosh of air as it lifts its airframe. However, it is not magic. The mechanics that make these birds soar are simple.

Inexpensive ARF foam models, like this GWS Spitfire, can be upgraded for more speed, maneuverability, and longer flights with brushless motors and Li-Poly battery packs.

ELECTRIC FLIGHT

The electric motor drives the propeller either directly (with the propeller bolted to the motor shaft) or through a gearbox, which provides more torque. The motor's speed is controlled by a solid-state device called an ESC. In order to make the motor speed up or slow down, its electronic circuitry transmits the pilot's commands from the on-board radio control receiver to the motor. The rudder, ailerons, and stabilizer flaps are controlled by tiny motors and gearboxes called servo motors, or servos. The power for all these comes from a rechargeable battery pack. To activate all devices, the radio receiver on the aircraft receives your commands from the handheld radio transmitter.

EFFICIENT POWER

The performance of model aircraft is affected by a number of factors including the efficiency or the aircraft itself, the model's total weight, the available power from the battery pack, the power of the motor, and the diameter and pitch of the propeller. In addition, the wind speed, barometric pressure, and relative humidity at the flying site (indoors or out). The ready-to-fly models have been engineered and tested to provide optimum performance with motor, propeller, and battery suggested (or supplied) by the manufacturer.

The ready-to-fly models are influenced by price constraints and performance. You can likely improve the performance of any ready-to-fly model by invest-ing in a lighter and more powerful battery pack with a more efficient motor and a propeller that matches the new motor. It is not at all difficult to spend more for the upgrades than you paid for the ready-to-fly model. Until you gain some experience through experimenta-tion, your upgrades may well result in a performance that is not even as good as the out-of-the-box model.

Josh Glavin flies the aerobatic 3-D flight and hovers an E-Flite Tribute with the tail inches from the runway.

ELECTRIC MOTORS

The lowest-priced toy flying model aircraft is usually powered by a can-style motor that is extremely inexpensive to produce and reasonably efficient. Hobbyists sometimes refer to these can motors as "ferrite," which is a rough description of the metal used for the magnets inside the motor. The more costly coreless motors produce more power and are relatively lighter than the ferrite motors. Both types have copper alloy brushes (like an old automobile generator) to deliver the current. Aircraft modelers sometimes refer these as brushed motors.

The most expensive motors are the brushless motors, named because they use an air gap to transfer the electrical current to the rotating armature. The brushless motors are well-suited for model aircraft because they draw far less power than conventional motors yet produce equivalent power. The brushless motors usually require a special ESC that has a different output than an ESC used for brushed motors.

There are several meters available to measure the amps, volts, and watts of a model aircraft motor including Astro Flight's excellent Astro Whatt Meter. Astro Flight also has a Model 100 Micro-Meter for the smaller aircraft that read from 0 to 15 amps in 1/10-amp increments. If you want an accurate measure of how much current the motor is drawing, you really need to check the current flow with motor, propeller, gearbox (if any), ESC, and battery installed in the aircraft. The maximum current draw when the motor is operating at full speed can be seen on the meter's digital read-out.

This AXI brand 22 212/26 is an example of the larger brushless motors. It sells for about $80.

Not all conventional or brushless motors draw the same amount of current for a given amount of power. The power alone is not the final answer. The overall weight of the airplane, the pitch of the propeller, and the use of gearbox can all have significant effects on how much power (how many volts and amps or watts) the motor may require for optimum performance. The motor's speed, or rpm, can also have a significant effect on how much power it will pull from the battery pack. With testing, you may determine, for example, that changing the pitch of the propeller can allow the model to perform better with less current draw.

The development of more powerful motors that consume less current is an ongoing process, where breakthroughs in power with minimum current consumption occur almost monthly. Recently, the most powerful motors have been the Astro Flight, Hacker, AXI, and nearly a dozen other brands of brushless motors. Thunder Power has complemented Hacker motors with a relatively new range of very large Li-Poly batteries that includes ones as large as 8200 mAh. The combination of brushless motors and Li-Poly batteries has allowed manufacturers and modelers to develop electric-powered aircraft that match the performance of the best fuel-powered aircraft.

THE GEARBOX

The motor you need for a particular aircraft will not always have the power and speed that is needed for the best propeller for that model. Many of the motor and propeller combinations will not have the power to pull the aircraft without a gearbox that will decrease the motor's effective speed (revolutions per minute) at the propeller. The right gear ratio will allow the motor to operate more efficiently and increase the amount of time you can fly on a fully charged battery pack.

Motor and gearbox manufacturers have charts to help you match the motor and propeller to the most efficient gear ratio. Generally, the gearboxes are offered in choices of 2.5:1, 3:1, 4:1, 5:1, or 6:1 ratios. The speed reductions means that motor will be turning 2.5, 3, 4, 5, or 6 times faster than propeller. Most of the gearboxes have simple spur gears that are designed to allow the propeller shaft to rest below or above the motor.

A few gearboxes, however, have planetary gears with small pinion gears that turn inside the larger gear. These gearboxes mount on the end of the motor,

Many of the motor and propeller combinations are more efficient if the motor speed is reduced with a gearbox like this 2.5:1-gear-ratio GD-600 from Electrifly by Hobbico. Copyright Hobbico, Inc., used with permission.

and some have about same diameter as the motor. The Astro Flight Firefly motor system has a pen-cell-size 7-watt motor with a 4:1 planetary gearbox (about same diameter as the motor), a 5x4 propeller, and speed controller in a single 16-gram package. The motor can be powered with a 6-cell nickel cadmium (NiCd) or 2S Li-Poly battery.

MOUNTING THE MOTOR

The replacement motor can usually be mounted in the same manner as the original motor. Few of the motors have any mounting brackets, so most are retained with clamps or rubber bands. If you need to devise a mount for a new motor, the easiest solution is to drill two 1/8-inch holes into the front bulkhead and/or the fuselage and use two 4- to 6-inch pieces of 1/8-inch carbon fiber rods, which you insert into the holes you drilled. The rods can be held in place with epoxy and should be placed about 1/4-inch closer together than the diameter of the motor so the motor rests on the rods. You can secure the motor with several heavy-duty rubber bands wrapped around the motor and the two rods.

Electric motors can create electrical interference that may partially block the radio signals to the receiver. To stop any interference, the motor must be protected with three small capacitors, like Radio Shack's 272-1065. The wires on the ends of the capacitors must be soldered in place. Solder one capacitor to one motor-connector wire and solder the other end to the opposite motor connector wire. Solder the second and third capacitors as grounds to the motor case, and connect one between the right motor wire and the motor case and the other between the left motor wire and the case. Most dealers can solder the capacitors for you (for a fee) if you don't know how.

FUEL-TO-ELECTRIC CONVERSIONS

Model manufacturers developed their models to fly with a specific motor and propeller, so it's wise to at least start with their recommendations. If you are re-powering a new (or older) fuel-powered model, you can only take a guess. Try to find an ARF or a ready-to-fly model that is similar in size and shape and weight to the model you want to re-power and buy the same (or one as close as possible to it) motor, gearbox (if one is suggested for the recommended motor), and propeller. Buy an ESC, transmitter, and battery pack to suit the motor.

PICKING A PROPELLER

The ready-to-fly and ARF models are usually supplied with a propeller that is just about perfect for that model. You can, however, often improve the model's performance by replacing the propeller with one that has a slightly larger or lesser pitch to suit the wind and climate conditions on any particular day at any particular flying site.

The propeller is sometimes referred to as an air screw because that is essentially how a propeller functions; it screws itself through the air. The propeller blade's angle or pitch determines how far it cuts through the air for each revolution. The pitch for model propellers is given as the number of inches the model could fly for each revolution of the propeller. The first number in a propeller rating is the propeller's diameter. Thus, a 7x4 propeller is 7 inches in diameter and will pull the model 4 inches for each revolution. A 7x8 propeller will pull the model 8 inches for each revolution.

The propellers intended for electric-powered aircraft are much lighter than those for fuel-powered aircraft, so be sure you buy an electric propeller. If the motor you are using requires a gearbox, you may need to purchase a different gearbox with a higher or lower ratio if you make a significant change in the propeller pitch. Your dealer can help determine the pitch of the propeller that is on your aircraft, and he or she may be able to recommend a replacement that might offer more performance for

your altitude and climate. Your best source of information about selecting propeller sizes and pitches are the folks at the flying field. They have probably tried half-a-dozen different combinations on a plane like yours and can help you get close to perfect the first time.

At present, variable-pitch propellers are only available for model helicopters. A number of clever modelers have adapted helicopter parts to create variable-pitch propellers, but it is something for the very advanced modeler. You can perform any aerobatic or 3-D maneuver with a conventional fixed-pitch propeller, assuming you have an aircraft capable of 3-D flights and the skill to accomplish them.

DUCTED FAN POWER

The ducted fan is the model aircraft flyer's answer to jet propulsion. A fan, usually with five blades, is used in place of a two-bladed propeller and is encased in a cylinder to provide some of the effect of a turbine, including 22,000 rpm fan speeds. There are ducted fan powerplants available for everything from park flyers to 10-pound giants. Most of the brushless motors can be fitted to the ducted fan engines so that you can have both power and light weight.

ELECTRONIC SPEED CONTROL

One of the breakthrough products that has enabled electric-powered aircraft to perform on a par with fuel-powered models is the ESC. The ESC translates the signals from the receiver to command the motor to speed up or slow down. These solid-state devices consume negligible power and are not much larger than a cigarette filter. The ESC must be matched to the motor's speed and power requirements. If you are using Li-Poly batteries, be sure that the ESC you select for your model is designed to be compatible with Li-Poly batteries. ESC units are available in sizes as small as 4-amp up to 77-amp capacity to handle the largest brushless motors.

Many of the ESC units are designed to be programmed with your laptop. The ESC makers and others offer programs for PCs. You may, for example, want to program the ESC so it precisely matches the motor's needs versus the power from the specific battery pack you have installed. You can program the ESC for the rate of speed-increase or to cut off the motor completely if the speed control is turned to zero.

Some of the ESC units include a battery cut-out (BEC) circuit to save enough battery power to operate

Some motor and propeller combinations provide the best performance with a gearbox like this one on the JustGoFly brushless motor.

This ICH400 from GWS is a typical ESC. The ESC is connected to the motor (left), battery (left), and receiver (right). This model also offers on-off switch control.

the radio system so you can land the aircraft safely. The circuit will automatically stop power from flowing to the motor when the battery level reaches a certain minimum. Some of the ESC units can be programmed for this minimum BEC and others have a preset level that will be indicated on the unit.

RECEIVERS

The receiver is the electronic device that translates the signals from the handheld transmitter into commands to control the motor and servos that move the rudder, elevator, and ailerons. Each of these functions requires a separate channel, so the larger models have four-channel receivers as well as matching four-channel transmitters.

The receiver's frequency must also match the frequency on the transmitter. Most receivers have a separate chip that must be removed and replaced to change channels, but some receivers, like Polk's Seeker II, automatically match the frequency from the transmitter.

Receivers are available in sizes to match the size and power requirements of the model aircraft. The FMA M5, for example, is a five-channel receiver for the park flyers and smaller aircraft and weighs 0.3 ounce. At the large end of the aircraft size spectrum, the FMA Quantum 8 has eight channels and weighs 0.5 ounce. Thimble-size servos for the smallest indoor fliers are available from Dynamics Unlimited and MicroMag.

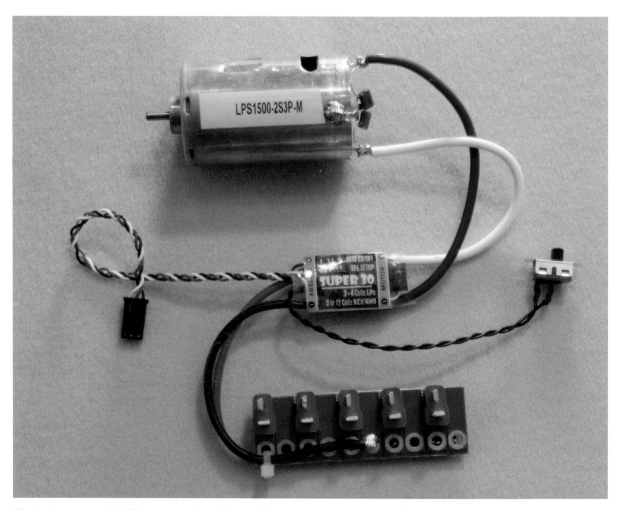

The basic motor and ESC connections with an FMA 600 Class motor 30 series ESC has an on-off switch (right), battery charger plug (left), and an FMA terminal strip (bottom) for connections of up to four servo motors.

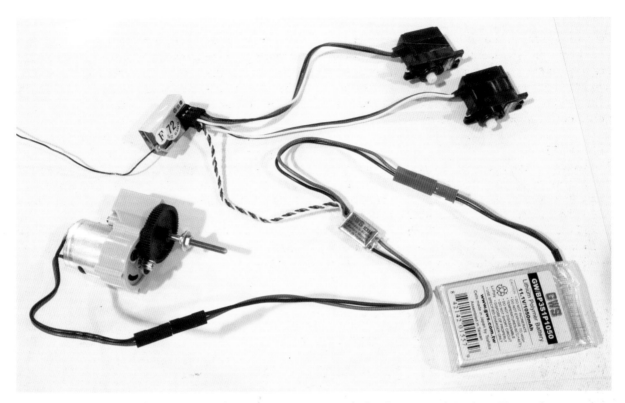

This is a complete electric power setup (clockwise from lower left): GWS motor and gearbox, 72-megahertz receiver with built-in on-off switch, two servo motors, and a Li-Poly battery pack. The ESC is in the center. Note that there are connectors for every component to make it easier to change out one component.

SERVOS

The rudder, elevator, and aileron flaps are moved through rods and cranks by small electric motors called servo motors, or servos. The transmitter sends more or less power to specific servo motors and/or reverses their direction. A crank is attached to the servo's motor shaft that pushes and pulls on a rod. The rod is connected to a protruding tab (usually called a control or horn) on the flap. When the servo motor turns one direction, it moves the crank, which pushes the rod that moves the elevator up. When the servo motor is commanded by the receiver to run in the opposite direction, the crank pulls on the rod to move the elevator down. All of the radio transmitters and receivers sold for hobby use—as opposed to the $100 or less toys—have proportional signals, which means that the more you move the control stick on the transmitter, the more the rudder (or elevator or aileron or motor) will turn. A smooth movement of the transmitter lever should result in an equally smooth movement of the rudder.

The servos used for electric-powered aircraft can be much smaller than those for fuel-powered aircraft or radio control cars. These smaller units are often called microservos and weigh about 0.02 ounce each. The microserver includes the usual motor, gear drive, and amplifier with a crank on top to accept the connection for the control rod that will move the rudder, elevator, or aileron flap. Most makers identify their servos by the electric aircraft category, so the smallest are Sub Micro or Micro, the medium-size aircraft models are park flyers, and the largest are Speed 400.

There are 1/2-inch square microservers available, including the GWS Pico and the WES-Tecnik LS-2.4, which are designed for 2- or 3-ounce Sub Micro and Micro aircraft. These devices weigh about 0.1 ounce.

The smallest servos are the dime-size magnetic actuators from Dynamics Unlimited and MicroMag. These are really just small magnets with wire coils that are mounted directly to the control surface. The actuators receive a signal from the decoding device attached to the receiver.

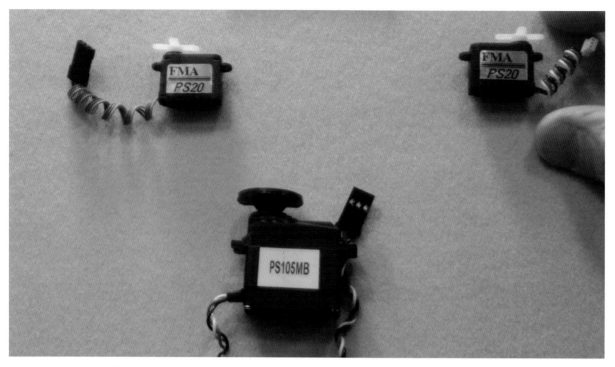

Several sizes of small servo motors are available for use in lightweight indoor models, like the FMA Direct PS20 (top right and left), as well as park flyers like the FMA Direct PA105MB with metal gears and ball bearings.

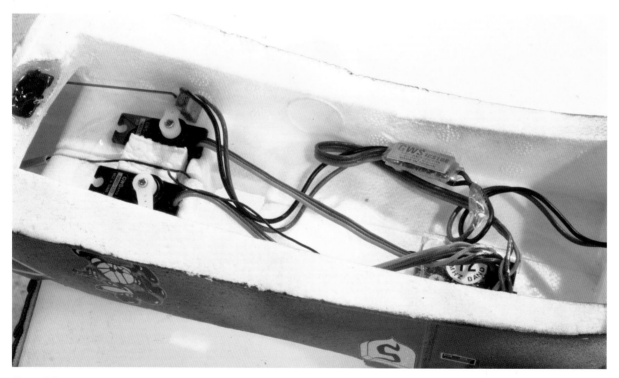

The ARF foam models, like this GWS Folke Wulf Bf109, have molded cavities to accept the two servo motors (left) and the receiver (far right). The ESC is the small yellow box. The battery pack will fit on top of these components. On this model the components are accessible by removing the wing, but other models may have a removable panel.

The ready-to-fly aircraft and most ARF aircraft include the servo motors and the control rods. On some you are expected to follow the instructions furnished with the model that inform how to attach the control rods to the servos and plug in the servos, receiver, ESC, and battery pack. If the model does not include servos, the instruction sheet will usually suggest two or three different brands that the manufacturer has tested to provide the best operation for that particular model.

The ESC is activated by one of the receiver channels to control the motor's speed. Most aircraft have two additional channels, one for the rudder and the other for the elevator. A servo is needed for the rudder and another for the elevator. These two are often mounted side by side near the center of the fuselage. Some kits have plywood brackets and other kits mount the servo on Velcro or double-stick foam. On larger models, a third servo is used to control the ailerons. A helicopter may have as many as six servos to control the rotor and tail rotor.

OUT-OF-CONTROL FLAP SLOP

The flaps on the rudder, elevators, and ailerons are called control surfaces for good reason: They control the aircraft. No flap should have any perceptible movement when the aircraft is at rest and the radio receiver is on. Any uncontrolled movement is called slop. If the flap can move freely for more than about 1/32 inch at its extreme rear edge, there is too much slop.

The servo should act as a brake to keep the control surfaces immobile. If the control surface moves without moving the servo or bending the control rod between the servo and the control surface, that slop can cause the aircraft to fly erratically.

Slop can also cause unpredictable responses to the controls. In some cases, slop can actually allow the control surfaces to flutter during flight, often with an audible buzz. That flutter will eventually weaken and break the hinges, which will make it difficult to land the aircraft without crashing. Slop can also result in very unpredictable control. You will usually want to adjust the transmitter levers so the

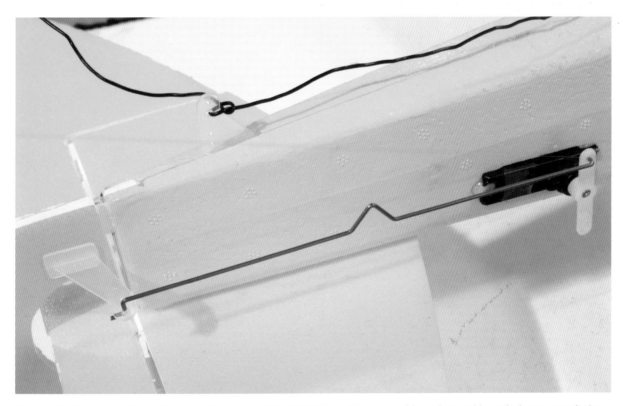

The control horns on the rudder and elevator on this GWS Tiger Moth are white nylon and have holes to attach the rudder and elevator. The squiggly wire is the antenna for the radio receiver.

aircraft flies straight with no pressure on the levers. With excessive slop, you can set the trim and release the lever, but after you have applied the control to move the elevator for a climb, leveled off the flight, and then returned the control stick to center, the aircraft no longer flies level.

If the model does not respond immediately to control input from the transmitter stick, it may because there is too much slop in the linkage. The receiver is telling the servo to move the control rod, and it does, but there is so much slop between the servo and the flap that it takes a few moments for the flap to move.

Ray Keeney set up his Ace Sim RC Carbon Falcon with a folding propeller and planetary gearbox on the motor (bottom). The two servo motors with white cranks to the wings are in the center, and the battery pack is in the front (top).

The control horns on the rudder and elevator of this Ikarus Shock Flyer are black nylon triangles with metal clips for mounting on the control rods.

Eddie Trujillo has installed pushrod connectors at the ends of the control rods. By loosening the set screw, the rod can be moved to provide correct flap adjustment with no slop.

A Giant Scale fully aerobatic aircraft may have six or more servos to control the rudder, elevator, and ailerons. These three servos actuate the rudder and elevators with a cable running forward to trigger the ailerons.

Ron Evans built this Playboy Jr. from an RN Models kit that was designed for a fuel-burning engine.

KILLING SLOP

The most common causes of slop are loose joints where the control rod attaches to the servo or where the control attaches to control surface. The lower-cost ARF and ready-to-fly models usually have a simple piece of steel piano wire with a Z-bend to attach the wire to the hole in the crank on the servo and the hole in the horn on the control surface. That wire is often free to rattle around in either or both of the holes, which it must be if there is to be no bind when the control is operated.

The most effective way to remove slop is to use pushrod connectors (small tubes with ball joints in one end) or clevises to attach the control rods to both the servo arm and the horn on the control surface. You can save weight by using carbon fiber for the control arms instead of steel piano wire. Pushrod connectors are available with 2-56 screws and thread into the 0.157-inch carbon fiber rods sold by Midwest and others. Bring the aircraft with you when you buy the pushrod connectors so you can be sure you get the correct sizes to match the holes in the servo arm and in the horns on the control surfaces. You may need to drill the holes to match the pushrod connectors, but a hobby dealer will have the correct size drill bit.

MATCHING THE MOTOR TO THE MODEL

There is the arbitrary measure of the motor's power, but there are no specific accepted parameters for motor size. Some of the manufacturers of motors provide their opinion of their motors' performance capabilities with a number code of 180, 200, 280, 300, 380, or 400. Generally a 180 motor is best for a 3- to 8-ounce Micro class aircraft, a 250 or 280 motor is most efficient in an 8- to 14-ounce parking lot, backyard flyer, and park flyer model. The larger aircraft in the Speed 400 class that weigh 18 to 30 ounces or more needs a 380 or 400 motor. Usually, the range of motors from any maker, whether conventional brush motors or brushless, includes all of these sizes.

You can do the math in order to provide a rough idea of whether the motor you propose to use has the power to even lift the aircraft. Power, in this instance, is measured in watts per ounce. Determine the motor's watt output from its specifications, or if you're using a digital meter, weigh the aircraft complete with motor, ESC, receiver, and battery pack as it would be when it's ready to fly. Divide the watts by the weight in ounces. Some very rough rules of thumb suggest that you will need 2.5 watts per ounce or more for an aerobatic or 3-D aircraft, but a powered sailplane can fly nicely with as little as 1.5 watts per ounce.

There are many other factors to consider in creating a successful combination of airframe, power, and weight, including wing loading and thrust. The variations are virtually infinite, but a computer will help. If you want to experiment further, I advise that you purchase one of the computer programs from ElectriCalc or MotoCalc.

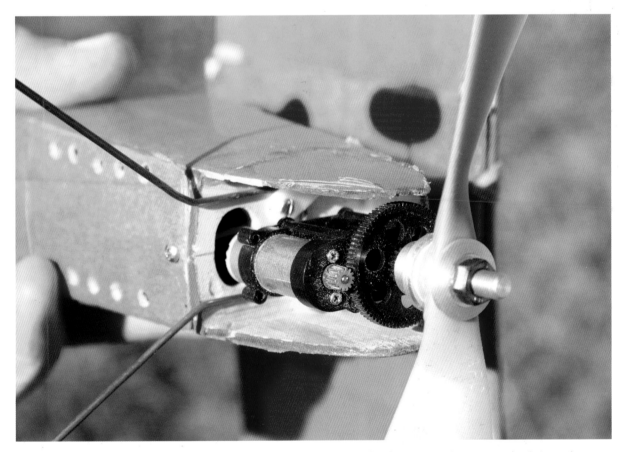

Ron Evans replaced the fuel-burning engine in his Playboy Jr. with a GWS 100 electric motor and a 6:1 gearbox. The gearbox and motor unit are mounted to a plywood front bulkhead with four long screws, which are hidden behind the large gear.

WING LOADING

Aircraft engineers and model aircraft enthusiasts refer to the amount of wing surface area compared with the weight of the aircraft as wing loading. The motor must have enough power to be able to carry or lift the wing loading.

To determine the wing surface area, average out the wing width by adding the width (chord) at the tip of the wing to the width (chord) near the fuselage and dividing by two. Then multiply the average wing width by the total wingspan. If you measured in inches, divide the answer by 144 to get square feet. For example, if a hypothetical park flyer has a 2-inch wing width at the tip and a 6-inch width near the fuselage, the average wing width will be 4 ([2 + 6] ÷ 2 = 4). The average wing width multiplied by the wingspan of 28 inches will provide the number 112, which will be used to calculate the square inch by dividing 112 by 114. Therefore the square foot wing area for this park flyer will be 0.778 inch.

If the total weight of this hypothetical model in a ready-to-fly state with battery pack onboard is 8.8 ounces, then the wing loading will be 11.3 (8.8 ÷ 0.778 = 11.3) ounces per square foot.

The aircraft with the lowest wing loadings are the easiest to fly, and conversely, the aircraft with largest wing loadings are the most difficult to fly. Beginning flyers will be better able to control model aircraft with a wing loading of between 5 and 20 ounces per square foot. Experienced flyers can learn to control models that are 20 to 40 pounds per square foot. Only experts should attempt to fly models with 40 pounds per square foot or more of wing loading. You cannot always design the model to achieve a wing loading, but you can improve the performance of any ARF or

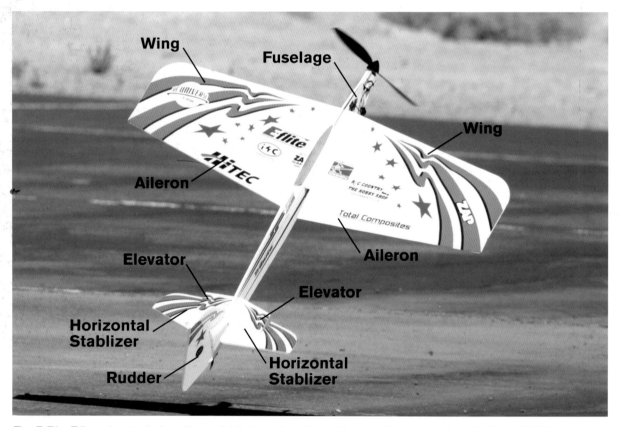

The E-Flite Tribute is a typical profile model that can be set up with enough power and control for 3-D flights. Working ailerons are not fitted to some of the beginner class aircraft.

The electrical components are mounted on the sides of the fuselage on the profile models like this Ikarus Shock-Flyer. The Li-Poly battery pack fits through a slot in the wing and a servo motor is mounted on either side of the flat foam fuselage.

Operating ailerons are needed in order to have full control over the model during some aerobatics, including inverted flight.

ready-to-fly model significantly with more powerful motors and/or lighter battery packs.

MOTOR/PROPELLER/ESC/BATTERY: A MATCHED SET

One of the secrets of electric-powered radio control aircraft is the balance between motor current needs, battery capacity, and the weight of the whole system. Several firms offer complete packages that may even include the receiver and servos pre-wired and ready to install.

There are packages for all sizes of aircraft, from the 3-ounce Sub Micro aircraft to the 30-ounce Speed 400 aircraft. FMA Direct, GWS, and others offer complete packages of low-voltage-draw receiver, ESC, and servos. The FMA Direct range has a compact package, with a Kokoham 120-mAh battery, ESC, a 3.7-volt receiver for Li-Poly batteries, and two servos, and this package works well for the most common parking lot- and backyard-size aircraft. The whole package only weighs about an ounce. Add the weight of the motor, propeller, and the aircraft itself and you could have a model as light as 4 ounces that can fly for as long as 20 minutes. There are, literally, hundreds of other possible packages.

COMPUTER—THE ANSWER FOR PREDICTABLE PERFORMANCE

The use of computers is another breakthrough that has made electric-powered flight possible. The variables that are induced into an electric-powered aircraft's system include choices of motor, propeller, gearbox, and the programmable ESC. There are two computer systems that have proven popular with flyers, the ElectriCalc (http://www.slkelectronics.com/ecalc/) and the MotoCalc 7 (www.motocalc.com/).

ElectriCalc was designed to take a lot of the mystery out of choosing the right combination of components for electric-powered models. It is user-friendly software that allows you to simulate an electric flight system for your model airplane with a battery pack, ESC, motor, gearbox, and propeller. It requires Windows 95 or a newer Microsoft operating system. If you are a Mac user, a PC emulator such as SoftWindows will run ElectriCalc. You can order ElectriCalc from your favorite dealer and download the ElectriCalc tutorial that is included with the program.

MotoCalc 7 is available for Windows 95, 98, ME, NT 4.0, 2000, and XP. MotoCalc 5 for Windows 3.1 and 3.11 is also still available. MotoCalc 7 gives the performance, duration, and flight characteristics. The program also predicts volts; amps; input and output watts; efficiency; temperature; watts/lb; rpm; thrust; pitch speed; and run time. You can use the program to test entire ranges of propellers, gear ratios, and numbers of cells at once to analyze hundreds of combinations in just a few seconds. MotoCalc 7 can also be used to predict in-flight performance over the entire flight speed range, including level flight time and the rate of climb (or sink) at any throttle setting from full power to off. With some experience, you can also make side-by-side comparisons of up to 10 results, whether with different motors, cells, or entirely different aircraft.

CHAPTER 4
Batteries—the Power for Flight

THE BATTERY is the fuel for an electric-powered model aircraft. Unlike liquid fuel used for internal combustion engines, the battery can be renewed by recharging. However, the batteries that have been adapted for use in electric-power model aircraft are often quite different from the rechargeable batteries you use around the house. These batteries require special care.

Smaller aircraft, like this GWS P-51D Mustang, can fly aerobatic maneuvers for up to 15 minutes if upgraded with a brushless motor and Li-Poly batteries.

BATTERIES
Essentially, a battery is a place to store energy. For model aircraft, you want the maximum amount of energy available with least possible amount of weight. The electric motor that powers the aircraft consumes most of the energy, with the servos that control the model drawing only momentary amounts of current.

Rechargeable batteries have become part of everyday life and have revolutionized model aircraft.

The battery chargers are now fast enough that you can recharge about as quickly as the batteries discharge. Purchase two battery packs and you can recharge one while you use the other.

You can determine a battery or battery pack's power-per-pound by dividing the watt-hours the battery provides by its weight. A battery analyzer can be extremely useful in determining how many watt-hours are available and how quickly that energy is dissipated for a given load.

The battery must be easy to install and remove so you can recharge it. The plug-in connectors must also be accessible. Hobby dealers offer a range of plugs and sockets that can be used with battery packs.

SUPER-LIGHT SUPER POWER BATTERIES

Battery weight is as much a problem as battery life for a model aircraft. A few years ago, the common nickel cadmium (NiCd) was as good as it got in terms of power-to-weight. More recently, nickel metal hydride (NiMH) batteries have become available that produce the same power with much less weight. The model aircraft industry has developed the NiMH battery packs and matching chargers, which produce the performance that makes an electric-powered model nearly match for the best fuel-powered aircraft.

The lightest batteries are the lithium polymer (Li-Poly) units. They are far more expensive than NiMH batteries, but they are also much lighter. The Li-Poly battery has truly made electric-powered aircraft a match for the fuel-powered models. The Li-Poly battery will power any type of motor, but the most efficient use of the Li-Poly's light weight is to combine it with the efficiency of a brushless motor. The brushless motor requires less current, so fewer batteries are needed for less weight. More often, modelers are satisfied with weight, but they want more power. Those modelers opt for a larger brushless motor to replace the stock brushed motor and use equally larger-capacity Li-Poly batteries. The net result is more power and more flying time with no more weight. But the Li-Poly battery and brushless motor combination is far more expensive.

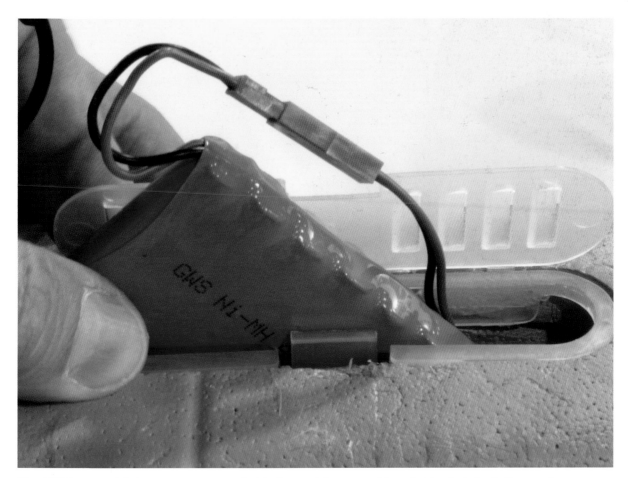

The ARF foam models have an extra space inside the model or a special pocket to place the battery pack.

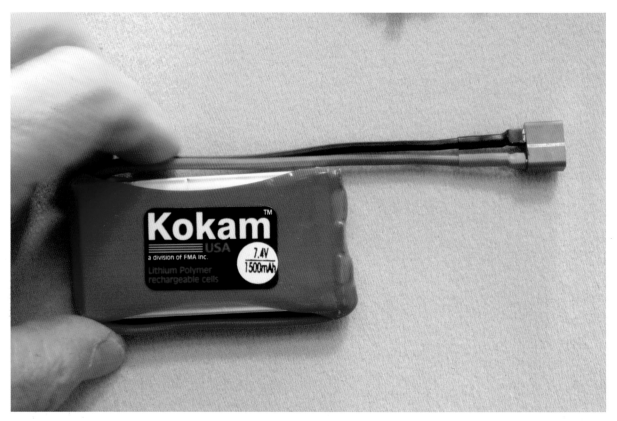

This compact Kokam Li-Poly battery offers 1500 mAh and 7.4 volts, enough to power most of the park flyer–size models for 15- to 30-minute flights.

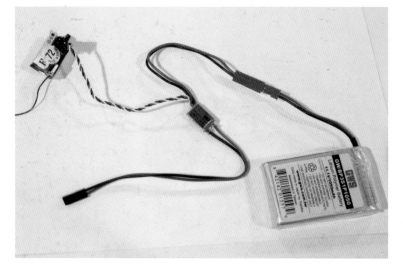

This is a typical electric circuit with a receiver (upper left), an ESC (center), and a compact 11.1-volt 1050-mAh Li-Poly battery, and the whole unit is about the size of half of a deck of playing cards. The red plug in the center leads to the motor and the servos plug into the receiver, while the black plug (lower left) is for recharging the batteries. The black wire in the upper left is the antenna. Complete installation is shown in Chapter 3.

One example of small Li-Poly battery pack is the Apogee from PFM Distributors. One Li-Poly Cells 7.4-volt 830-mAh battery is about the size of a pack of matches. It is listed with a 10-14C discharge rate, which is shorthand for a 1050-mAh cell that can be discharged at about 14 amps. In actual use, a battery pack this size will usually have a usable capacity of about half that or 720-amp-hours at 4 amps.

Today, the most common uses for Li-Poly batteries are for the very lightest and heaviest electric-powered aircraft. A brushless motor with a matched-to-the-motor NiMH battery pack is state-of-the-art for the vast majority of experienced model aircraft flyers.

The Li-Poly battery pack in this Ikarus Shock Flyer fits through a slot in the wing, and a servo motor is mounted on either side of the fuselage.

The yellow-covered NiMH battery pack on Chuck Shafer's GWS DeHavilland Beaver is slung from the bottom fuselage with rubber bands.

LITHIUM POLYMER BATTERY HAZARDS

The American Model Aircraft Association (AMA) has issued a warning about the hazards of Li-Poly batteries. The principal risk is fire, which can result from improper charging, crash damage, or shorting the batteries. A Li-Poly battery burns at several thousand degrees. Fire occurs due to contact between lithium and the oxygen in the air. It does not need any other source of ignition or fuel to start, and it burns almost explosively. These batteries must be used in a manner that precludes ancillary fire.

The AMA recommends the following information:

1. Store and charge in a fireproof container—never in your model.

2. Charge in a protected area devoid of combustibles. Always stand watch over the charging process. Never leave the charging process unattended.

3. In the event of damage from crashes, carefully remove the model to a safe place and observe for at least a half hour. Physically damaged cells could erupt into flames and, after sufficient time to ensure safety, should be discarded in accordance with the instructions that came with the batteries. Never attempt to charge a cell with physical damage, regardless of how slight.

4. Always use chargers designed for the specific purpose, preferably with a fixed setting for your particular pack. Many fires occur because of improper use of set selectable/adjustable chargers. Never attempt to charge lithium cells with a charger that is not specifically designed for charging lithium polymer cells. Never use chargers designed for NiCd or other types of batteries.

5. Use charging systems that monitor and control the charge state of each cell in the pack. Unbalanced cells can lead to disaster if a single cell overcharges in the pack. If the batteries show any sign of swelling, discontinue charging and remove them in a safe place outside because they could erupt into flames.

6. Never plug in a Li-Poly battery and let it charge, unattended, overnight. Serious fires have resulted from this practice.

7. Do not attempt to make your own Li-Poly battery packs from individual cells.

These batteries CANNOT be handled and charged casually, which has been the practice for years with other types of batteries. The consequence of carelessness can be very serious and result in major property damage and/or personal harm.

BATTERY CHARGERS

You will likely need at least two battery chargers for your electric-power radio control aircraft: one to charge the batteries for the transmitter, and another to charge the batteries that power the electric motor and radio control gear inside the aircraft. With today's electric-power aircraft, one battery pack is usually used to power the motor and radio control receiver, ESC, and servos.

CHARGING NICD AND NIMH BATTERIES

It is well worth the money to invest in a $100-plus battery charger that will detect when the battery is at full charge and automatically shut itself off. Trickle chargers can easily overcharge or undercharge and thus shorten battery life. The charger must also be designed for the specific batteries you are charging. Most can be switched back and forth from NiCd to NiMH, but some are designed to charge only one type. The Astro Flight 110D is one example of a peak detect charger that can charge up to 18 NiCd or NiMH battery cells with up to 5 amps of charge current. The Hobbico Triton (from Great Planes' Electrifly line) will also charge NiCd or NiMH batteries.

The battery chargers offer some fail-safe protection for charging, but you must also apply some common sense. If a battery has become dented, water-soaked, or damaged in any way, throw it out. Never attempt to charge a damaged battery. Often, the batteries will be hot after a flight from the relatively rapid discharge. The batteries must be cool to the touch before recharging. You can speed up the cooling process by buying a small 12-volt fan (to plug into the cigarette lighter outlet).

CHARGING LI-POLY BATTERIES

There are several battery chargers that are designed to charge Li-Poly batteries. The Kokam 502 charger is available from FMA Direct and Ikarus. This charger will handle up to five Li-Poly batteries in a series, with up to 2.5 amps. The charger is powered by a 12-volt DC current. The Kokam 502 will bring a completely discharged Li-Poly battery up to 90 percent charge in about an hour. The Astro Flight 109, Great Planes Electrifly Polycharge, and the Multiplex Multi Charger LN-2010 are also designed to charge Li-Poly batteries.

Kokam offers two Safety Guard devices; one for two Li-Poly batteries and the other for three Li-Poly batteries. The Safety Guard is inserted in the wires between the charger and the battery to prevent over-charging, mischarging, and explosions.

The compact MC2002 charger from GWS is designed to charge only NiCd or NiMH batteries.

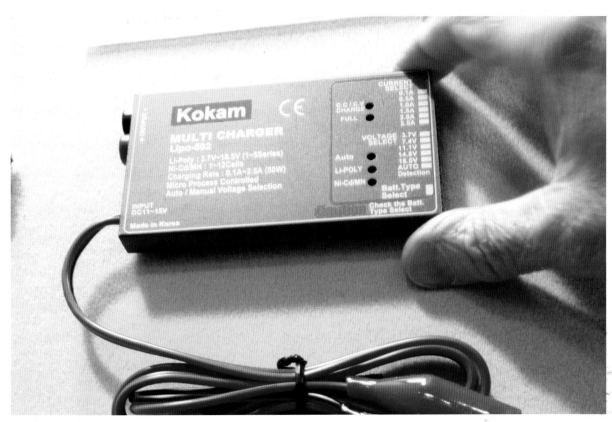

The Kokham 502 charger from FMA Direct and Ikarus will handle up to five Li-Poly batteries in series, with up to 2.5 amps. The charger is designed to be powered by 12-volt DC current.

The Hobbico (Great Planes' Electrifly brand) Polycharger is designed to charge Li-Poly batteries. Copyright Hobbico, Inc., used with permission.

BATTERY-LIMITED FLIGHT TIME

When the aircraft's on-board battery pack goes completely dead, your model is out of control, and in all probability, lost to the four winds. Before the model is launched, you should know for certain that the transmitter and aircraft's on-board batteries are fully charged, and it's wise to have a fully charged replacement set nearby just in case. You should also know exactly how long the model can fly with a fully charged battery.

Many of the ESC units have a BEC circuit that will stop power flow to the motor and leave enough current to operate the flaps for a return flight. There may even be enough current for a short burst of power to accomplish a perfect landing.

There is no way to determine precisely how long the model will fly because there are a near-infinite number of variables, including how much power you need, which is going to vary with how much throttle you use, which is also affected by the wind. You can, however, calculate how much current the motor will need if you have to spend the entire flight at full throttle.

You cannot do a dry run to test the model on the ground because it will overheat the motor and ESC. The result would be completely inaccurate anyway because the motor is not really working to pull the aircraft through the air.

The motor will usually have a label indicating its maximum current draw. That information may also be in the instruction booklet furnished with model. You will also be able to read the maximum fully charged capacity on the battery pack. Let's say the motor has a maximum rating of 1.2 amps and the battery pack is rated at 150 mAh. Express the 150 milliamps in amps, which is 0.15, and multiply that by 60 (minutes in an hour) to get 9, then divide that by the motor current ($9.0 \div 1.2$) and the answer is 7.5 minutes of flight time. Not much, but you will seldom use full throttle for the entire flight. You can also use these same calculations to determine how much longer the flight might be with a more efficient motor.

THE FLIGHT DIARY

How much longer you can fly after the mathematically calculated fail-safe time is something you can only determine with experience. The better battery chargers will have a display that indicates the remaining life of the battery, so you can determine how much time you have left after any flight and you can record that information in a flight diary.

Keep a flight diary notebook and record the details of every flight, including the duration, a good guess at the speed and direction of the prevailing winds and any other climate changes that might affect the flight, and a note on how much battery life remained after the flight. With the experiences recorded in that notebook, you will be able to get a much more accurate picture of how long you can fly with any aircraft/motor/battery combination. You can use that information to make some good guesses for other aircraft, and it can be helpful when and if you decide you want to upgrade the model with a more efficient motor and/or a lighter battery pack.

BATTERY TESTING

There are several battery analyzers available to help you determine how any given set of batteries will perform. The West Mountain Radio computerized battery analyzer (CBA) provides line graphs to show the potential battery power with amps, volts, watts, and amp-hours. With it, you can actually see how quickly the battery or battery pack will discharge under the load of the motor and radio gear. The CBA includes the hardware to connect the battery pack to your PC.

The battery analyzer program is a way to balance the output of your choice of motors to the batteries you have available. You may, for example, determine that a NiMH battery pack provides enough performance, or that you really do need to install a Li-Poly battery pack to get the flight duration you desire. The West Mountain Radio CBA also has an optional temperature sensor with an automatic overheat-cut-off that can minimize the danger (to both the battery and yourself) from rapidly discharging batteries. Experienced fliers feel that the maximum temperature for a rapidly discharging battery should be no more than 140 degrees Fahrenheit (60 degrees Celsius). Stop any performance tests immediately if the battery is near that temperature.

With computer programs like the West Mountain Radio CBA, you can create individual specification and performance files for each of your battery packs. Label the files with date of purchase and update them in your flight diary with subsequent flights and/or battery discharge tests so you have a recorded history of each battery pack. The dates will help you determine how well the battery is maintaining its original power, as well as provide a benchmark for later charge/recharge cycles.

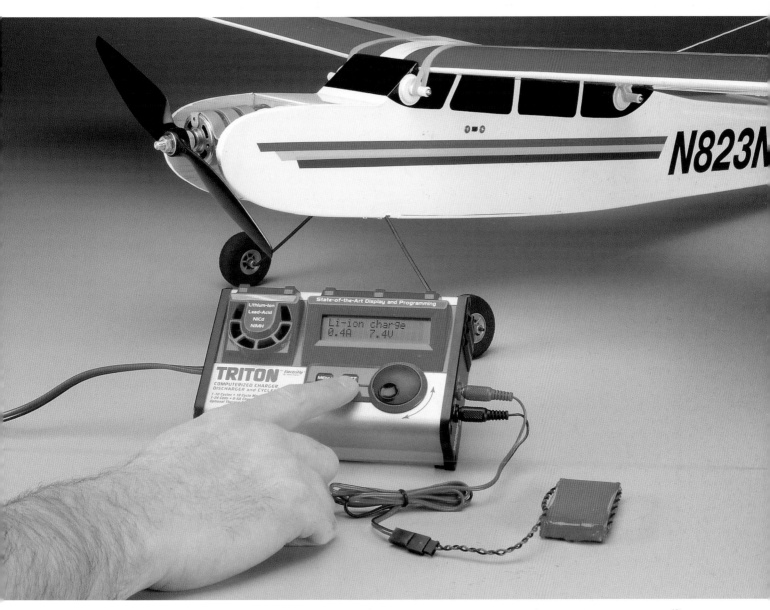

The Hobbico Triton (from Great Planes' Electrifly line) will charge Li-Poly, NiCd, or NiMH batteries.

CHAPTER 5
Control, by Radio Control

THE TERM "radio control" is intended to describe how the commands from the pilot are transmitted to the model aircraft. You (the pilot) still have to learn how to move the levers and switches that relay your commands. The radio transmitters used for model aircraft have one or two levers that can be moved up, down, right, or left in a manner similar to a joystick on a real airplane.

Radio control provides a method for you to translate your desires of which direction the aircraft may take into commands the aircraft will follow.

RADIO CONTROL TRANSMITTERS

A transmitter is likely to be the single most expensive purchase you make in the hobby, so it is a commitment to a future of flying fun. I would recommend that you purchase the best transmitter you can afford so you can keep it for all the future models you may want fly (including helicopters). Airtronics and Futaba are two of the top-of-the-line brands, but others (like Polk's Tracker III with selectable channels) have specific advantages. Winners of various flying competitions have used about every brand including Futaba, Airtronics, Polk's, GWS, JR, Hitec, Lexors,

Megatech, ParkZone, HobbyZone, Tower, and others. You can probably get the best advice on which transmitter to buy by talking to the folks in your local flying club, but you should do some research on your own to decide which transmitter would best meet your specific needs for now and in the foreseeable future.

It's certainly not a waste of money to have more than four channels, even if your model only needs two or three. Eventually you will want to fly aircraft where you have more control than what is offered with just two or three channels. Having stated that, there's nothing wrong with buying a package that includes an inexpensive transmitter and a ready-to-fly aircraft as your flight trainer. The more expensive and sophisticated transmitters will also fly the least expensive aircraft, so you can continue to fly your first model aircraft for decades or until you can no longer repair the aircraft.

Only the two- and three-channel radio control transmitters like those supplied with the ready-to-fly packages of aircraft and transmitter and the lower-priced transmitters like the Futaba Skysport SS-3/3FR or Hitec Focus III SS have a single joystick. On these transmitters, the control for speed is usually another knob or slide switch.

Radio control transmitters with four or more channels usually have two joysticks, and the second stick is used to control the model's speed and rudder that allow the model to turn. For controlled aero-batics and 3-D flight, you need four channels to control the rudder, elevator, ailerons, and motor speed. The six channel transmitters are only necessary if you also want the option of dropping fake bombs, lowering the landing gear, or launching a glider from the aircraft. You also need a six-channel transmitter for the larger helicopters.

The toy radio transmitters with only two channels might have a range as short as 750 feet. Some of the lower-cost transmitters have a 1,000-foot range. The more powerful three-, four-, five-, and six-channel hobby transmitters can transmit reliable signals as far away as a mile. Actually, stray signals can travel as far away as three miles, but for predictable control, consider about a half a mile the limit. Frankly, that's farther than most of us can see, but the extra range can provide enough control necessary to recover an out-of-control aircraft.

This JR model XP9303 nine-channel transmitter is needed only for a 3-D helicopter, but the precise control makes it easier to fly any aircraft, especially an upgraded 3-D airplane like this Ikarus Shock Flyer.

Polk's Hobby offers a six- or eight-channel Tracker III radio control transmitter (and matching Seeker II receiver) that will allow you to select any frequency without changing a frequency chip in either the transmitter or receiver. Courtesy Polk's Hobby

THE TRANSMITTER AS A CO-PILOT

The better radio control transmitters offer a trainer socket on the side of the unit to allow another transmitter to be plugged in. The second transmitter can be used by your flight instructor to override your controls in order to save your model from a crash. It would be wise to spend a few hours at the local flying site and talking to your local hobby dealer about the hobby before investing in a transmitter or an aircraft model. Try to determine if there are club members who would be willing to help you learn to fly. Also, find out if one of your potential flight instructors has a radio transmitter with the trainer capability and buy a transmitter that will function with your flight instructor's transmitter. Later, when you become an experienced flier, you may become the instructor for a newcomer.

COMPUTERIZED TRANSMITTERS

The more expensive radio transmitters, like the Futaba 6EXA, Polk's Tracker III, Hitec Optic 6, JR XP9303, and others, have built-in programs that allow you to program a variety of special control settings and adjustments. You can program the transmitter to save both the exact adjustments of the controls and the specific combinations of controls. Customized programs can be extremely helpful when flying aerobatic models in 3-D hover or knife-edge maneuvers. You can determine the best control settings for a 3-D aerobatic airplane and program that as "3-D," and then fly your favorite helicopter and program the fine-tuning adjustments for it. When you go back to flying the 3-D airplane, select your own customized "3-D" program. The larger transmitters have enough memory for up to 30 different aircraft settings.

Top-of-the-line transmitters, such as Futaba's 14MZ, offer 14 channels. You can set up as many as six trim tabs on a giant powered sailplane or ducted-fan jet and program the best settings for each. Memory is stored on a 32MB compact flash card. The Futaba 14MZ has a full-color computer screen with large displays for in-flight data like time and channel selection. The screen can make it easier to program custom control settings. The transmitter also has adjustable verbal prompts.

RADIO CONTROL FREQUENCIES

The radio control signals are carried on specific frequencies so that the only radio receiver in your airplane will respond to those signals. The Federal Aviation Administration (FAA) has assigned frequencies in the 72 to 73 MHz primary band to modelers. There are 50 discreet or dedicated channels available in that range for flying models, from channel 11 to channel 60. Each model aircraft flying field has a flight board, usually with 50 color-coded and numbered clothespins to match each of the 50 frequencies. Any missing clothespin is the indication that another flier is using that frequency.

When you enter the flying area of the field and are prepared to fly, you grab the clothespin from the flight board that matches the frequency of your transmitter and receiver(s). You should clip it your transmitter's antenna to make it easier for the official to find you and your frequency, and to help you remember to return the clothespin to the flight board when you are through flying. That effectively prevents anyone else from using the same frequency. Your responsibility is to use only that frequency and to return the clip to the flight board as soon as you are through flying. If you have a radio with another frequency, you must select the clothespin to match

It's helpful to find an experienced flyer to teach you the nuances of radio control.

that frequency and return it when you are through. Some of the more sophisticated transmitters have adjustable frequencies so you have a choice, and the same rules apply.

The lower-priced radio control transmitters have a fixed frequency, while the medium-priced transmitters have a removable chip so you can buy an optional frequency. Buy a matching receiver.

Although 50 frequencies are available, usually only 12 or so are usable because transmitters are often supplied with a few popular frequencies. You should ask your dealer to be sure your transmitter is not one of a dozen he has sold with same frequency. If so, ask him to order a transmitter or crystal with another frequency. It is possible to change crystals in either the transmitter or the receiver, but it's not that easy.

There are surprisingly few mid-air collisions, but you must be absolutely certain that you are operating on the correct radio frequency and are the only one on it.

Each of these four flyers has complete control of their aircraft, thanks to dedicated radio frequencies for each radio transmitter and receiver.

The flight board (left) has clothespins with radio frequency numbers and matching positions on the board. This is the board used at the NEAT Fair in New York.

Many clubs have a simple pole for a flight board, like this one (upper center) at the Rocky Mountain E-Flyers site in Arvada, Colorado.

Note the clothespin on the radio transmitter aerial that identifies the radio frequency this flyer is using at the NEAT Fair.

If you are buying a six- or eight-channel transmitter, you might consider one that has adjustable frequency control like the Polk's Tracker III. This transmitter can be adjusted to any of the 50 frequencies by turning a knob.

OVERCOMING THE "RIGHT-AT-YOU" DISORIENTATION

You'll discover that it is relatively easy to control a model aircraft when the model is moving away from you. If you think about it or if you have actually flown a model aircraft, you will realize that the model is flying toward you almost half the time. Even when the aircraft is flying past you, heading right or left, it will be coming toward you until it passes your position and only then will it be heading away from you.

When the model is flying toward you, the control-input must be reversed right-to-left. The words are simple, but you'll need to learn to retrain your reactions and to adjust your reaction to the rudder control stick. What is not so obvious is that you will also need to adjust your reaction to the aileron control if you want to bank the aircraft or rotate around the fuselage axis in a roll aerobatic maneuver. Even speeding up the motor can be confusing if you are used to pushing forward in the direction the aircraft is flying for more speed. When the aircraft is flying toward you, you must push toward the rear of the aircraft. The disorienting part is that the radio transmitter does not move with the airplane so your fingers must make any corrections. There are at least three techniques you can try to find out which one works best for you.

It is easy enough to know which lever to push in order to turn the aircraft right or left when it is flying away from you.

Some pilots keep their body turned in the direction the aircraft is flying. Thus, when the aircraft is coming toward you, you are facing your body away from the model with your head turned so you can look over your shoulder. It's awkward, but it can be helpful for a new flyer because it keeps your connection between the ground and the aircraft. You can keep the transmitter oriented in the same direction as the aircraft. I have never met an experienced model aircraft pilot that uses this technique, although a few admit to trying it when they were new to the hobby.

Some model aircraft pilots prefer to imagine themselves inside the cockpit of the aircraft. They remain facing the model at all times. The trick with this technique is to disconnect yourself with ground mentally so you are flying up there with model. Most pilots I have talked to find themselves imagining they are in the cockpit for most of the flight.

The third technique is the one that most experienced pilots seem to prefer. When the model is flying toward you, you will want to alter its path. Decide which way you want it to turn and simply push the rudder control stick in that direction. Ignore any

When you turn the aircraft and it flies at you, the rudder control lever direction is reversed; you push left to turn right.

concept of being in the cockpit and push the stick the direction you want to turn the model. You can ease into this one by applying just a touch to the controls to barely move the aircraft. Then if the aircraft responds by heading the way you wish, simply apply more lever movement.

THE ACADEMY OF MODEL AERONAUTICS

The AMA is a self-supporting, nonprofit organization. Its purpose is to promote the development of model aviation as a recognized sport and worthwhile recreation activity and it is open to anyone interested in model aviation. The AMA is the voice of its membership and provides a liaison to the FAA, Federal Communications Commission (FCC), and other government agencies through its national headquarters in Muncie, Indiana. The AMA also works with local governments, zoning boards, and parks departments to promote the interests of local chartered clubs.

As the official national body for model aviation in the United States, the AMA sanctions more than 1,000 model competitions throughout the country each year and certifies official model flying records

The incredibly quick aircraft with brushless motors, like this upgraded Hanger 9 Twist, includes controls for the ailerons that allow the model to be banked right or left or maneuvered in rolls and Immleman turns, as shown in Chapter 8.

This Twist is heading upwind on a landing approach, but it will be flying toward the pilot until it flies past him.

on national and international levels. This is the world's largest sport aviation organization and represents a membership of more than 170,000 people from every walk of life, income level, and age group, and is the chartering organization for more than 2,500 model airplane clubs across the country. AMA offers its chartered clubs official contest sanctions, insurance, and assistance in obtaining and keeping flying sites.

The AMA is the organizer of the annual National Aeromodeling Championships, the world's largest model aircraft competition, and is an associate member of the National Aeronautic Association (NAA). Through NAA, AMA is recognized by the Fédération Aéronautique Internationale (FAI), the world governing body of all aviation activity, as the only organization that may direct U.S. participation in international aeromodeling activities.

It also offers members insurance including commercial general liability coverage; accident; medical; and fire, vandalism, and theft coverage. The insurance can be especially useful when establishing a club flying site and for holding competition events.

The Academy of Model Aeronautics (AMA) chapters stage thousands of flying meets and competitions each year, like this one in Las Vegas. There is usually an early morning pilot's meeting—like this one—to establish which channels are being used and to describe the itinerary of the day's events.

CHAPTER 6
Preparing for Flight

IT IS NEVER SAFE to assume that a model aircraft is ready to fly. If you have assembled the aircraft from one of the quick-build ARF kits, you have made some choices about receivers and servos, and perhaps more of the components, and your model appears to be ready to fly. Before you head for the flying field, take time to perform all of these pre-flight checks.

A pilot and his spotter are doing 3-D maneuvers on the flight line at the 2004 NEAT Fair.

BALANCE POINT SETUP

Most aircraft models include an instruction sheet that indicates where the balance point of the model should be. Usually the center of gravity (the balance point) is just forward of the main spar of the wing, but it can vary a few fractions of an inch. The model must be balanced so neither nose or tail droops during flight. To check the model's balance point, install all of the electronic gear, including the battery pack and any devices, like FMA Direct's Co-Pilot, that you might have added. Hold the model with two fingers at the center of gravity. On some high-wing models you may actually need to hold the model on your fingertips at the wing's spar.

If the fuselage is level with the propeller at exactly 90 degrees to the ground, then the aircraft is balanced correctly. If the tail hangs down, you can sometimes move the battery pack forward until the balance point is perfect. Conversely, a nose-heavy model can be adjusted by moving the battery pack toward the rear of the model. Be sure to install a new battery pack mount (with a relocated mounting bracket and thick rubber bands or a pair of Velcro strips) to secure the battery in the new position. In some rare cases, just moving the battery pack is not enough, and a small amount of weight must be added to the nose or tail. Attach the weight to strongest part of the model's structure, like a rear tail skid or the motor mount. You can use a self-adhesive 1/4-ounce lead balance weight, which is used for real automobile wheel balancing, and cut the weight in half or in fourths. When you have the balance weight where you want it, attach it firmly with epoxy.

RADIO TRANSMITTER AND RECEIVER CHECK
Always make a pre-flight check of any aircraft before you pack up and head for the flying site. Prepare the model so that it is completely ready to fly with all batteries fully charged and installed and everything working properly. You may need to make emergency repairs at the flying field, but it's easier to work on the model at home. Turn the radio transmitter on and check the operations of all the controls.

Firstly, be sure that the stick or lever that controls motor speed allows the motor to operate through its full range while a friend holds onto the model to keep it from taking off. The motor should increase its speed when you push the stick away from you (on four-channel radios). Do not take anything for granted. With the motor running, be sure there is wind behind the model to ensure that the motor is turning in the right direction and that the propeller matches the motor.

The Esprit Sokol can be upgraded to a competitive pylon racer with a Hacker Competition Carbon motor and a 1300-mAh 3-cell Li-Poly battery, like Jorge Castorena's model.

This GWS DeHavilland Beaver model has a GWS EPS-400C motor, ICS 300 ESC, GWS R4P receiver, three GWS NARO mini servos, and a GWS 9.6-volt 730-mAh NiMH battery pack.

The Hanger 9 Twist, as set up by Glen Crowzer, has a Hacker C40 motor with a Castle Creations Phoenix 80 receiver and a 2600 Li-Poly battery pack.

The GWS models, like this Tiger Moth, can be purchased with a complete set that includes low-cost GWS brushed motor, ESC, receiver, servos, and NiMH battery pack.

The Ikarus Shock Flyer, as set up by Dan Loris for the NEAT Fair in 2004, flies nicely with an AXI 22 08/34 motor and Li-Poly battery. He also reinforced the wing's leading edges with carbon fiber strips.

Frank Dilatush's Kyosho Spree is an ARF model. The NiMH battery pack was replaced with a lighter Li-Poly battery pack located slightly further forward to maintain the model's center of balance.

The balance point (center of gravity) on this powered sailplane is just behind the forward edge of the wing. This is also the point where you hold the aircraft to launch it by hand.

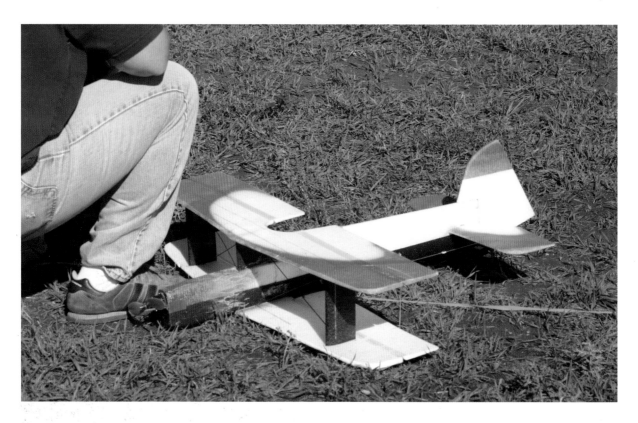

The entire stabilizer, not just the rear elevator, tilts up and down on the Northeast Sailplane products' 2Cool. Frank Dilatusch is testing the radio control operation of the stabilizer as part of his pre-flight check.

Test the controls for the rudder; be sure that the transmitter's trim lever is adjusted so the rudder is in the straight-ahead or neutral position with the left-hand control stick in the centered position. When you move the rudder control stick to the right, the rudder should move right (looking down the fuselage toward the nose). Repeat a similar check with elevator controls to ensure that the elevator moves up when you move the stick toward you and down when you move the stick away. If you have a four-channel transmitter, the controls for the ailerons will be on the right stick. When you move the stick to the right, the right aileron should move up and the left aileron should move down. All of the control surfaces should be perfectly in line or neutral when the control sticks are at their mid-points. Most transmitters have adjustments so you can zero-out the control sticks.

Check the operation of the rudder, elevator, and ailerons to be sure they respond at the speed you expect as you work the transmitter control sticks. If there are exponential (fine tuning) adjustments for speed of responses on the transmitter, you may want to use them to get the feel of what you can expect.

Josh Glavin is holding his transmitter in his left hand while he makes a final check on the rudder, aileron, and elevator controls in a final pre-flight check on his E-Flite Tribute.

AIRCRAFT INSPECTION

Inspect the assembled aircraft to be sure that the wings, stabilizer, and rudder are not warped. You can look down the wing from one end to determine if the far wing tip is in alignment with the wing tip closest to you. Repeat this inspection on the stabilizer. Look down the fuselage from the nose to tail to be sure the rudder is in line with the fuselage and is at right angles to the stabilizer. Also be sure that the wing tips are equally higher than the tips of the stabilizer.

Check the model for any loose parts. The control surfaces should work freely but should not be so loose that they can rattle. Be sure all the control rods from the servos are free to move without excessive rattle so there is no slop, and be sure the attachment control horns on the rudder, elevator, and ailerons are firmly attached. This is a good time to turn off the motor and check the propeller's nut and motor mounts to be sure they all are tight. Be sure the ESC, receiver, and battery pack are mounted securely.

A small tool box can contain the tools and cements you need to keep flying even after minor crashes.

Ron Evans does a final pre-flight check for smooth motor response to the transmitter controls.

SIXTEEN-POINT PREFLIGHT CHECKLIST

One of the first lessons you learn when obtaining a license to fly a real aircraft is to check the aircraft before you fire it up. That is also true of models. Once again, the experienced model aircraft pilots at the local club's flying site are your best instructors. Most will rundown a checklist similar to this:

1. Check the transmitter to determine if you are the only user of your chosen frequency.
2. Check the transmitter's range by walking at least 50 paces away from the model while operating the transmitter. You can ask a friend to watch the aircraft to see if the controls respond correctly.
3. Check the condition of the battery in the transmitter.
4. Check the condition of the batteries on the aircraft.
5. Check the operation of the motor by using the transmitter to control its speed while a friend holds the model securely.
6. Use the transmitter to check the operation of the rudder. Watch the rudder's action and inspect the hinges and the mechanical linkage to the servo to be sure everything is working freely and that the hinges and links are not worn or cracked.
7. Check to be sure the rudder moves in the direction you expect (right for right turns, left for left turns) when you move the control stick.
8. Check that the rudder moves at the speed you expect so you won't accidentally overcorrect (respond too fast) or not be able respond quickly enough.
9. Repeat number 6 with elevator control surfaces.
10. Repeat number 7 with the elevator control surfaces.
11. Repeat number 8 with elevator control surfaces.
12. Repeat number 6 with ailerons.
13. Repeat number 7 with ailerons.
14. Repeat number 8 with ailerons.
15. Hold the model at its center of gravity to see if its fuselage is parallel to the ground, indicating that the center of balance is correct.
16. Wiggle the motor, propeller, battery pack, and the landing gear to be sure all are firmly attached.

WHAT TO BRING TO THE FLYING SITE

It may seem obvious, but remember to bring the entire aircraft. Some of the larger models have detachable wings, and you would not be the first to leave the wings at home. You will also want bring all of the items suggested in Chapter 11 (which covers maintenance and repairs), including a tool kit.

You may want to take your laptop computer to reprogram the ESC unit for specific flying conditions, for it might dictate a change in propeller or battery pack. The laptop can also be useful if you are experimenting with different combinations of propellers, motors, and/or battery packs to obtain maximum performance.

Give some thought to your personal comfort at the flying site. A large brim hat, sunglasses, and sunscreen are basics. You might also want take binoculars to watch other aircraft in flight. A lounge lawn chair can be a heaven-sent when your neck tires from being bent backward for so many hours. You can lie back and watch the flights. You may also want to bring a cooler with refreshments and a trash bag to clean up after yourself. Some flyers bring umbrellas or small pop-up canopies. Finally, bring a fire extinguisher because a severe crash can damage the batteries or rip wires to cause a short or a small explosion.

Ron Evans has a flight box with yokes to hold the model (two pairs of wings, in this case). He uses a milk crate to carry additional radio gear and parts to the flying field.

CHAPTER 7
Flying Lessons

THE FANTASTIC models displayed in these pages were not designed to hang from a string or sit on a shelf. First and foremost, these are flying machines. Their beauty is usually a forms-follows-function—some really do fly as well as they look. Not one of them, however, is designed to fly all by itself. It's up the pilot (that's you) to draw out the maximum potential from each model. Flying a model aircraft is most definitely a learning experience and something that will only be perfected with practice.

You have two possible classrooms to use in learning how to fly a model aircraft: Take the model to the flying site and fly it or use a computer-generated flight simulator.

The safest way to get your model airborne is to launch it by hand into a gentle wind.

LOCATING A FLIGHT SCHOOL

There are no formal flight schools that I know of for learning to fly model aircraft. If you have guessed that it's easier to learn to fly a model airplane than a real one, you are correct. However, there are many more maneuvers that you can perform with a model airplane, so the real experts in model aircraft flight are highly trained, skilled individuals who have practiced for hundreds of hours.

The more experienced model aircraft pilots usually gather together at the nearest club flying site.

You would be wise to find out where and when they meet for three reasons. Firstly, there is almost always someone at the flying site who is willing to help you learn. Sometimes the club owns a few model aircraft that it maintains just for beginners (like you) to use to learn to fly. Secondly, you need to know where the others are flying so you do not interfere with their flights or vice versa. Third, there is no lesson more valuable and no flight simulator as realistic as having an experienced pilot talking you through the movement of the control sticks and levers for those first few flights.

The flying field should be marked with a flight line to keep pilots from wandering onto the landing area. The pilot positions at the NEAT Fair are identified with 2-foot-high orange plastic fences.

It is easier to learn the launching technique if you have an experienced pilot help you by manipulating the transmitter controls so you can concentrate on getting the perfect launch.

FLYING SOLO

If you are learning to fly a real aircraft, you will spend hundreds of hours with a second pilot sitting at a second set of controls. With a model aircraft, your first flight will be solo. You can, however, get some help. An experienced model aircraft pilot is usually available at a club flying field.

Your "flight instructor" may simply stand behind or beside you to tell you which control to use, and in some cases, to move the controls for you. If you did your homework, you may already have discovered if the transmitter your flight instructor is using has a trainer capability and can be plugged into your transmitter so that he or she can help you learn on the site. If both your flight instructor's and your transmitters have trainer ports, the two transmitters can be connected by a special cable. The flight instructor can then allow you to perform all the controls without any help. If you are about to enter into an out-of-control crash maneuver, he or she can push an override button and assume instant control of your aircraft through the master transmitter.

One of the advantages of today's electric-powered aircraft is that most are relatively lightweight, which means there is less chance of massive damage. Modern foam construction, especially when reinforced with carbon fiber, also makes today's flying models very resistant to crash damage. You probably will break a few propellers while learning, so it's a good idea to take along a few spares.

Watch for other low-flying aircraft whenever launching a model.

Most flying sites will have a windsock or a flag to provide an indication of the direction and strength of the wind.

FLIGHT SIMULATORS

There are several flight simulator video games. These are interesting, but are of very little help in learning to fly radio control model aircraft. The model aircraft manufacturers have developed several variations of true radio control flight simulators. Some of the least expensive units have their own simulated radio control receiver. A few allow you to use your own transmitter.

These flight simulators project a model aircraft—often an exact replica of the airplane or helicopter model you want to fly—on your computer's monitor screen much like in a video game, but you use an actual radio control transmitter to maneuver the aircraft on the screen. You are literally using your own radio control transmitter to fly a virtual model aircraft. Many of the manufacturers of model airplanes and helicopters offer flight simulator CDs for specific model airplanes and helicopters, including MRC's Reflex XTR RC, Great Planes' Real Flight, Ikarus' Aerofly, and others.

The flight simulators are especially helpful in learning the complex controls of larger aircraft that may have many control surfaces and for learning the nuances of flying a helicopter. The flight simulators that allow you to use your own radio transmitter allow you to get a feel for how quickly and how far to move the transmitter controls in order to achieve the desired effect on the aircraft's performance.

It's certainly less traumatic to crash your simulated aircraft than crashing the real thing. Once you have mastered the basics on the screen, apply those hand-eye coordinated experiences to the sticks on your transmitter to control the actual model aircraft. You can practice operating the transmitter controls in your backyard without actually flying the model. Start by moving the levers that activate the control surfaces so you can see, close-up, how the various flaps respond. It takes a lot of flying experience to understand just how far a flap needs to move in order to achieve the desired change in the aircraft's flight attitude, so don't try to memorize the cause-and-effect of your finger actions until the aircraft is actually in flight. Work the controls for the motor, rudder, elevator, and ailerons, just as you did when "flying" with the simulator. Watch how the model's components respond to various quick and slow movements of the control sticks on the transmitter and how much each moves as you move the control sticks.

MAINTAINING CONTROL FOR RADIO CONTROL

The first rule of flying by radio control is to never assume, no matter what, that you are alone with your radio transmitter. There may be someone flying an radio-controlled aircraft 3 miles away, and if he or she is using the same radio frequency you are, your aircraft is going to be completely out of your control. Many of the more expensive radio control transmitters and some of the receivers—like the FMA Direct co-pilot-equipped receivers—emit a signal to tell you if any other transmitter is currently using the radio frequency you have selected, but they are only effective when the other user is operating (as would be a radar detector for your car). The AMA has a zip code listing of flying and racing sites which can help. You can also ask all the local hobby dealers where the nearest flying or radio control sites may be. Do not assume just because you are in a large area that you are in control. Really, the safest sites are those used by the local model aircraft clubs.

If you have never used radio control before, you might consider installing one of the auto pilot devices like the Co-Pilot from FMA Direct. The Co-Pilot is a 1-ounce add-on electronic device (similar to a helicopter's gyro) that can be used with any radio receiver, and FMA Direct also offers a range of radio receivers that include the Co-Pilot circuitry. Essentially, the Co-Pilot automatically brings the model back to level flight and maintains that altitude until it receives a radio-transmitted command from your frequency to adjust any control. The Co-Pilot will not save your aircraft from some other flyer using the same frequency, but it will bring the aircraft back under control when you have lost control. The Co-Pilot can be installed inside the aircraft or it can be attached to the exterior on the bottom of the aircraft at the center of gravity. It also includes a plug and socket so you can remove the Co-Pilot and install the unit on another aircraft.

I strongly recommend that you practice using your radio control transmitter before you head for a flying site. Get used to how the joystick feels and what pressure and degree of movement you need to apply to get the motor to respond and the flaps to move through the full range. Understand that every transmitter is going to provide a slightly different feel from the next, even when the sticks on both operate the same functions. If you have more than one transmitter, you will need to spend at least a few minutes to get used to the performance of whichever one you are using for the current flight.

Hold the receiver in your non-dominant hand (your left if you are right handed). Hold the aircraft at its center of balance so that you don't need to worry about the nose or tail dropping.

Set the rudder control slightly right to offset the torque from the propeller. Do not turn the speed control to full power until you are ready to launch the model.

With full throttle and slightly up elevator, the model should almost fly out of your hand—give it a strong throw as you might lob a softball. With most aircraft, throw the model up at about 10 to 15 degrees from horizontal, as Frank Dilatusch is doing.

FLYING FIELDS

Your local electric model aircraft club probably already has both outdoor and indoor flying facilities. If you have to find your own site, locate one that is as far away from houses as possible. Sometimes there are soccer fields and other open areas in industrial parks that make perfect flying fields on weekends. The size and power of the aircraft you will be flying determines how large a field you will need. The majority of the electric-powered models can be flown in an area as small as baseball diamond (including the airspace directly above that baseball diamond). The larger and faster aircraft need an area about half the size of soccer or football field, while electric-powered sailplanes are more fun when they are flown in areas several times that size. Obviously you must adjust your flying schedule to match the not-in-use periods of any soccer field. If you are using a private lot, you need to obtain permission from the owners. These are things that the local club will have already done for you.

When you are flying with others, establish a mutually agreed flight line, such as the edge of the grass or some other defined straight line (you can mark it with caution tape or a day glow rope if necessary). All of the flyers should agree to stay behind that line and within an imaginary box about 6 feet square so you don't accidentally bump into another flyer. It's also wise to limit the flights to the area behind the flight line—fly directly overhead and to the horizon line you are facing, but never behind your back or behind the backs of the other flyers. This is a common sense safety precaution for both the other flyers and for any spectators. If you brought your own cheerleaders, instruct them to stay behind the flight line.

GETTING AIRBORNE

Virtually all model aircraft are designed so you can fly them from a smooth grass flying field or a parking lot. It will be far less frustrating learning how to take off from the ground if you can learn on a smooth parking lot or dirt road. Most flying fields are far from smooth, especially for the relatively small landing wheels on a model aircraft. At most flying sites, you will need to learn how to hand-launch the aircraft and allow the lumpy grass to slow and catch it on landing. One of the local model aircraft club members will usually be willing to hand-launch your aircraft a few times to show you the technique and then walk you through it so you can learn for yourself.

Determine the direction of the wind by checking a nearby flag or wetting your finger and feeling which side is the coolest. Always launch the model into the wind. When launching the model, hold it as near as possible to the center of gravity and keep the wings level. Do not attempt to launch it upward more than about 10 degrees or it may stall. The built-in lift from the wings should get the aircraft moving. Image the model to be like a softball and lob the aircraft—there's no need to try to make a fastball pitch. Just send it off much as you may when imitating a fly fisherman casting. You can also take three or four running steps to add a bit more air speed to the launch.

There's a special thrill in watching a takeoff from a taxi run, which you can perform if the ground is smooth enough. You will discover that torque from the propeller will force you to set the rudder slightly right to keep the model taxiing straight. If the model is a tail dragger, you will have to move the elevator up a bit to keep the tail on the ground until the model has reached takeoff speed. Conversely, with a nose landing gear tricycle, you may need to add a bit of down elevator control to keep the nose on the ground until the model reaches liftoff speed.

Try taxiing back and forth a few times and gradually increase the throttle to get the feel of how the airplane reacts and how much you need to change the rudder and elevator controls to keep the model running straight. This also gives you a chance to see how you react to the model coming toward you, as opposed to moving away from you. When you're comfortable, try a takeoff into the wind and increase the throttle gently, but steadily, to full-on and slowly add more up elevator control to get the model airborne. Let the model assume a fairly steep climb, somewhere between about 20 and 30 degrees from horizontal and under full throttle.

Dave Hock's GWS F4U Corsair has a Himax 350C motor, a Tobrey 3.9:1 gearbox, and a 10/8 propeller, so it has plenty of power for a steep (about 30 degrees from horizontal) upward launch.

Dave Hock gives a flick of his upper arm and wrist to get his high-powered Corsair into the air.

Frank Dilatusch's Northeast Sailplane 2Cool has an upgraded motor and Li-Poly battery, which makes it is powerful enough to pull itself up at a steep (almost 45 degrees to the horizon) angle. Launches this close to vertical are risky because the model could stall and you don't have much altitude to catch the stall before the aircraft crashes.

As soon as the model is airborne, Frank will remove a bit of elevator angle to maintain a somewhat shallower climb to the desired flying altitude.

WING TIP LAUNCHES

Some of the larger 60-inch hand-launch-powered sailplane models can be fitted with pins to allow wing tip boomerang launches. A 3- or 4-inch-long, 1/8-inch-wide piece of carbon fiber rod can be attached with epoxy vertically about an inch in from the end of the wing. The rod must also be linked to the rest of the wing with a wing-length strip of carbon fiber about 1/4- to 1/2- inch wide. The carbon fiber spreads the load of the launch through the wing and the fuselage so the steel pin is not ripped from the wing tip.

Hold the pin between your second and third fingers and make a V using those two fingers to grip the pin on the top and bottom of the wing. Move your body as you would when hurling a discus. Essentially, you spin on the inside foot, using the outside leg and foot to propel your body 360 degrees around your inside foot. Extend your arm with hand holding the tip of the wing as you rotate your entire body as quickly as you can through the full circle.

An experienced launcher can propel the model up to 60 miles an hour before it leaves his or her hand. Relax the grip of those two fingers when the aircraft is heading in the direction you have chosen. With this technique, you can launch the model upward about 30 to 45 degrees. With a slight breeze, the aircraft can reach an altitude of 100 to 150 feet. With practice and a few adjustments on the transmitter, you can get your model to fly on its own for several seconds, which is long enough for you to reach the transmitter and apply the controls you wish.

The traditional electric winch or hi-launch (rubber band launchers) for non-powered sailplanes can also be used with electric-powered radio control aircraft. However, the presence of an electric motor (and propeller) for power makes the need for such powerful launchers unnecessary.

Powered sailplanes can be launched by gripping a carbon fiber pin mounted through the tip of one wing, like this one on Allan Wright's sailplane. Grip the pin as shown to launch the model.

Use a full-body spinning movement, much like you would use to throw a discus, to launch the plane. The whipping action of your arm and the spin of your body can get the model moving up to 60 miles per hour as it leaves your hand.

THAT FIRST FLIGHT

You can decide if you want to take off from the ground or if you want to hand-launch your first flight. If you are confident enough with taxiing, give that a try. For the first hand-launch, it can be helpful to have an experienced flyer launch the model so you can concentrate on working the transmitter. Once you are comfortable with that, you can add hand-launching it yourself. Some flyers leave the transmitter on the ground while hand-launching, but most hold it in their opposite hand (with a tether around their wrist so they don't drop the transmitter).

For your first flight, launch the model upward about 10 degrees from horizontal with the elevator set at neutral. Let the model fly straight for about 100 feet and it will likely gain altitude with minimal up elevator control. When the aircraft is about 100 feet in the air, level off its flight with less up elevator control. Make a gentle right turn, followed by another 50 feet

of straight flight, and then a second right turn, this time flying with wind and past you. Make a third right turn, followed by another 50-foot straight, and a fourth right turn to head back toward you and into the wind. As soon as the aircraft is level, add some down elevator control to begin a descent for a landing.

Flight time is a learning period. Try decreasing and increasing the engine speed to see how it affects the aircraft and learn how to adjust the rudder, elevator, and/or aileron controls to maintain level and straight flight at different air speeds, when turning left and right, and when accelerating or decelerating.

POWER-FADE TELLTALES

You must to land your model before the battery becomes completely discharged. You need enough reserve batter power to apply a bit of motor power to keep the nose up when landing, and perhaps even enough energy to abort a landing and try again once or twice. There is really no fail-safe method of knowing when the power is fading. The experienced flyers in the local club can fly with you and help you determine when you should stop flight. Experience (and some of the battery life-check systems) can tell you about how long the model should be able fly on a single charge. You can perform a rough check by applying a burst of throttle every five minutes during the flight to see how quickly the aircraft responds. Perform those "power checks" with the aircraft flying at about the same speed and into about the same amount of wind each time. If the response is sluggish, even relatively early in the flight, bring the aircraft to a safe landing and check the battery's charge. It may just be unusual wind conditions, or you may be using more throttle (and battery power) than you expected.

AVOIDING STALLS

One of most common causes of a loss of control with an aircraft, be it model or real, is a lack of enough power to complete a maneuver, causing the aircraft to stop flying or "stall" in midair. Sometimes, the aircraft simply does not have enough power or the pilot did not apply enough throttle or, if the pilot did, then he or she did not applied soon enough. Most often, however, stalls are caused by the pilot applying too much "up" elevator. Reducing the amount of up elevator will often correct a stall much faster than any increase in power. It does, however, require some practice to learn which control is going to provide the quickest recovery.

Stalls are a common hazard when you are learning to land a model aircraft. Learning to land begins with learning to maintain full control under straight and level flight. With the model flying at about 100 feet and level, slowly decrease the throttle until the model stalls, then try to recovering with just a bit more throttle to catch the stall before it takes control. You'll need that experience when landing.

A LANDING IS NOT A CONTROLLED CRASH

I once had a commercial pilot tell me that landing a jet plane was really a controlled crash—it only seems that way when it bounces. Regardless, the most difficult part of learning to fly a real airplane is the landing. It is far easier to land a model aircraft because the relatively thicker air (compared to the size of the aircraft) helps buoy and support the model.

To land any aircraft, it's safest to head into the wind as much as possible. For a beginning flyer, it's even better to land with no wind at all. You will be far less frustrated when you are learning to fly by radio control if you wait for a day with little or no wind. Electric-powered flight has a major advantage over fuel-powered flight because the electrics are silent. That means you can get to a flying field at dawn when wind is usually the most still. The only noise any neighbors will hear will be you shouting in joy after having successfully completed your first flight.

When you are learning to land, make the first few landings on a paved or smooth dirt surface. Once you have learned how to apply just enough rudder and throttle and when to cut the throttle, you can advance to applying those lessons to landing in a grassy field. Nearly all model airplanes will flip nose foreward when the ground speed is low enough. The clumps of grass are just too "grabby" for the lightweight aircraft to roll. Stubby grass in the 2- to 6-inch range is the most difficult, and taller grass can actually serve as a skid pad to allow the model to slide and float along with tall grass suspending it above the hard ground. It will eventually nose over, but the grass cushion and slow speed should prevent any damage to the model. Most plastic propellers and most motor mountings are strong enough so that the propeller should not be broken or the motor ripped from the model if the plane noses over at something less than a walking pace.

PRACTICING "SAFE" LANDINGS

One of major causes of crashes on landing is the pilot's misreading the aircraft's ground speed. Often the crash is caused by too little ground speed. When you are learning to land when there is a wind, it can be useful to practice flying some oval patterns with 100-foot or longer straight legs between each 180 degree turn. Use the oval patterns to simulate a landing, but level-off about 50 feet above the ground to get a feeling for how the wind is affecting the aircraft as it changes from upwind to downwind. The safest way to learn to land is to make the 180 degree turn with the aircraft flying level so you are simply turning and not attempting to lose elevation as well. When the turn is complete and the aircraft is heading upwind (flying into the wind), begin the descent.

Try a few more rectangular laps around the flying field at about 40 feet, then at 30 feet, and notice about how much more throttle you need to

The best place to learn how take off from the ground is a stretch of pavement or sidewalk so the model won't bounce or pitch unpredictably.

When taking off from a grassy field, the elevator must be slightly up to keep the tail wheel on the ground and the propeller from hitting the grass. When the taxi speed is fast enough, gradually release the elevator control.

Some aircraft can be landed with no power, but it is risky. It's best to have power available to pull the nose up just as the aircraft touches down.

maintain a given ground speed when heading into the wind. Usually you will find that the lower the aircraft flies, the more throttle is needed to maintain the same ground speed when heading into the wind. Even with a slight wind, there can be a significant difference the closer the aircraft gets to the ground. Learn to land by making the path with the wind a bit longer than you might estimate so you have plenty of room to make a full 180-degree turn back into the wind with no abrupt changes in rudder or elevator control.

There's no reason why you cannot make a half-dozen rectangular laps, losing altitude only on the straight legs of the ovals, until the aircraft is flying around just 10 feet or so above the ground. As the aircraft gets close the ground, back off on the throttle to let aircraft soar or flair, but be prepared to apply more up elevator and perhaps even more throttle to maintain ground speed into the wind until the aircraft has landed safely and smoothly.

FLY LIKE THE WIND

Murphy's Law dictates that the wind will only be unpredictable when you are least able to cope with it. The majority of these model aircraft are extremely stable and most can be flown successfully and under complete and precise control even with mild winds or mildly gusty winds. Yet even mild wind can produce a variety of flying conditions that can make it almost impossible to control the aircraft if you are not aware of what is happening. For starters, the wind is almost always blowing harder the higher up from the ground. If you are taking off, you may discover that the model assumes an ever-increasing nose-up attitude the higher it gets, even with no additional input on the elevator control. The wind is literally lifting the aircraft at an increasing rate as the aircraft enters areas of stronger wind currents. Landing in relatively stiff winds can be more problematic because the aircraft will tend to drop the nose the closer it gets to the ground because the wind is decreasing. If you are landing into a stiff wind, be prepared for less wind as the plane descends and counter that with additional amounts of throttle to maintain control.

GROUND SPEED VERSUS AIR SPEED

The speed that an aircraft travels is often referred to as air speed, and the instruments in the real aircraft provide that reading, which is not available for model aircraft. However, if there is wind, the aircraft's actual speed is going to be increased by a tail wind or decreased by a head wind. The wind alters the aircraft's true travel time, which is referred to as ground speed. If you are just flying around 200 or 300 feet off the ground, the difference between air speed and ground speed is not important. You can make up any effect the wind has on the model's flight by applying more power when heading upwind or spending a bit more time heading upwind than down to keep the model more or less overhead.

You can sample the wind while the aircraft is flying by setting the rudder and elevator controls so the plane is in a steady circle. With no wind, the plane will fly in a near perfect circle. With wind, the plane will be pushed by the wind to fly in spirals as the wind pushes the plane in its path. In the air, the aircraft is still making perfect circles but it is covering more distance on the ground as the wind pushes it along. Use that experience to determine how much the wind is pushing the aircraft off its intended course so you can make the necessary corrections in the control levers to fly the flight path you desire.

CHAPTER 8
Aerobatic, 3-D, 4-D & Combat Flying

ONE OF THE JOYS of flight is to be able to maneuver the aircraft completely at will through the air with little apparent regard for "up" or "down." Roils, loops, figure eights, and similar maneuvers are usually described as aerobatics.

When the aircraft climbs with the wing inside the loop, the maneuver is called an inside loop.

LOOPS
Loops are perfect circles performed vertically. A loop is one of the basic aerobatic maneuvers that is used, with variations, for Immlemann turns, split-S turns, and more complex aerobatic maneuvers like figure eights.

A simple loop begins and ends with the model flying in the normal attitude. Since no inverted flight is involved (except to a brief moment at the top of the loop), you can accomplish this maneuver with a simple three-channel transmitter. When the top of the wing always faces the inside of the loop, this is called an inside loop.

Begin the loop with the aircraft flying into the wind. Some aircraft need more air speed than is possible with full throttle. With those models, you may need to begin the loop with a shallow (less than 30 degrees from horizontal) dive to gain air speed. You will have to practice the maneuver to determine when the aircraft has reached an adequate speed to complete the upward half of the loop. Apply the up elevator control gently to ease the aircraft into its upward path. The aircraft loses speed as it climbs so you need to experiment with how tight a loop it can make (and for how far it must climb) to have the power to complete the first half of the loop. Since there is a likelihood that the model may stall when you first attempt a loop, it's a good idea to have an experienced pilot at your side to help you make the corrections necessary to bring the model out of a stall.

When the aircraft begins its descent for the second half the loop, its air speed will automatically increase. It's wise to slowly back off on the throttle to maintain a fast flying speed on the second half of the loop. Keep the elevator control set until well after the model has reached level flight so it will not dive when you release the elevator to resume level flight.

For competition, the loop must be as perfect to a circle as possible, with the aircraft beginning and ending the loop at same point. Also for competition, the loop may also include a full 360-degree roll with half the roll being accomplished on the upward half loop so the aircraft is flying in the normal manner (wing down) at the top of the loop. A second 180-degree roll is accomplished as the aircraft dives downward to complete the loop so the aircraft resumes a normal flight position at the end of the maneuver.

Learn to begin and end the basic aerobatic maneuvers with level flight.

THE LOOP.
This is the simple loop maneuver with the aircraft beginning and ending in normal, level flight.

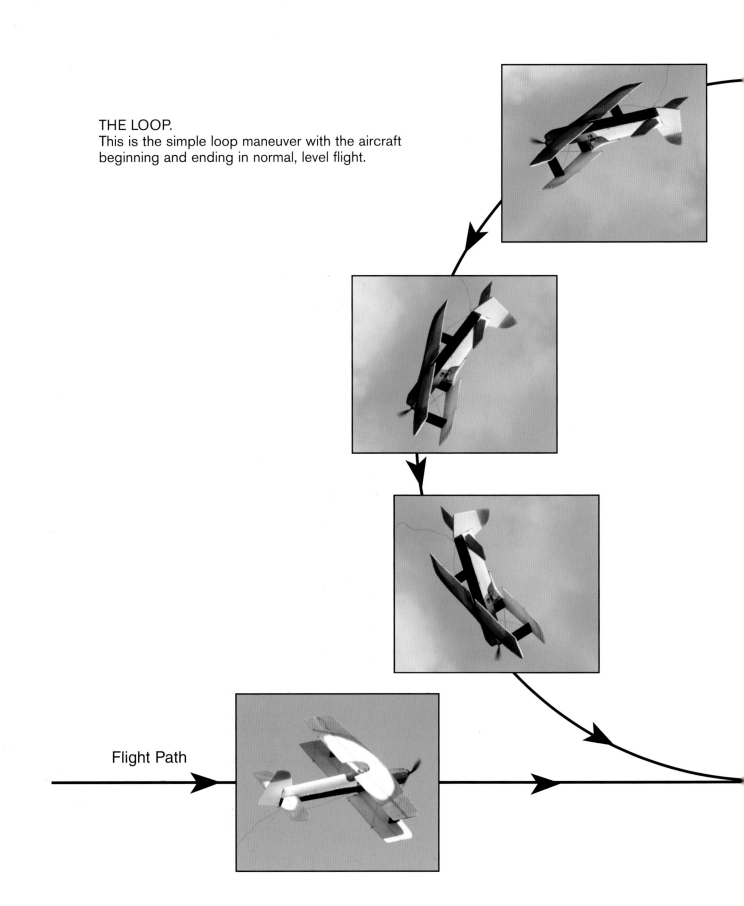

Flight Path

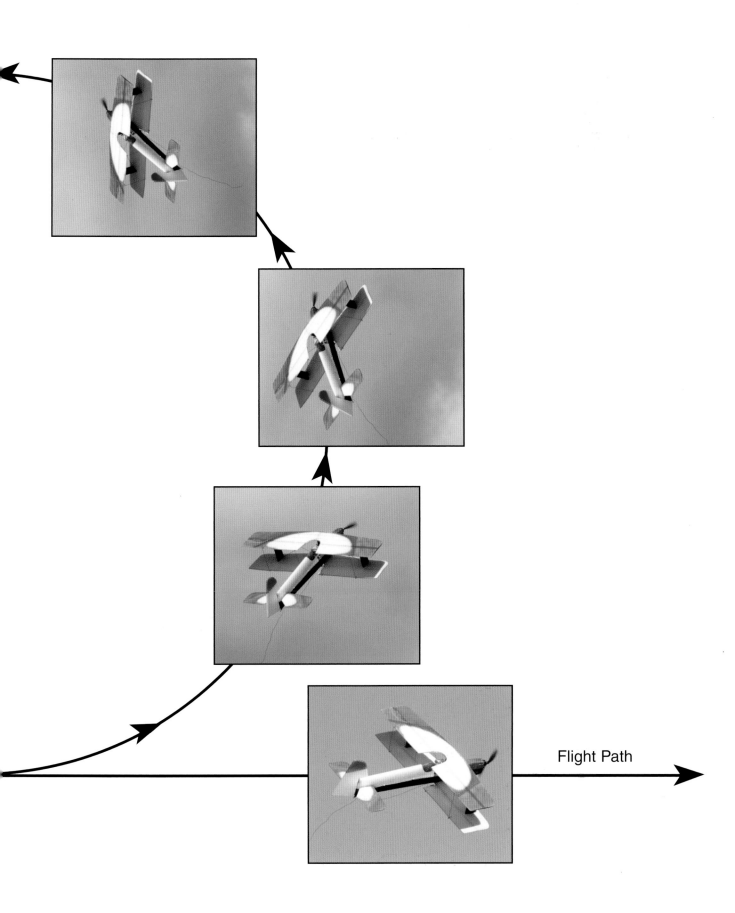

Flight Path

Josh Glavin flies a series of rolls over the Nevada desert mountains.

INVERTED FLIGHT

One of the more exciting aerobatic maneuvers is flying the aircraft upside down or inverted. Inverted flight can be dangerous because the elevator control inputs must be reversed. When you want the model to gain altitude during inverted flight, you move the stick to provide down elevator.

It is possible to achieve inverted flight with a three-channel system by performing half of the loop maneuver but allowing the model to continue flying inverted when it reaches the top of the loop. When you are ready to bring the model back to the conventional flight position, complete the second diving half of the loop. With a four-channel radio system and an aircraft fitted with ailerons, inverted flight can be accomplished by executing a half-roll.

Some model aircraft that do not have ailerons can be forced into a rather ragged roll. Most models are designed to automatically bank when the rudder is moved. You can use the built-in design to force some models to roll. Apply full right rudder and full up elevator at once. The model should virtually flip over in the air. That's the easy part—you'll need to repeat the process to bring the model from its inverted flight back normal flight. Be sure you have at least 100 feet of altitude before attempting to flip the model back when using full right throttle and full elevator control, because it will likely dive for the earth at about the same time. Once again, it's wise to have an experienced model aircraft pilot at your side to help you accomplish inverted flight without using ailerons.

ROLLS

Only aircraft with ailerons on the rear of the wings can accomplish a smooth roll. The aircraft's servo motors should be installed so that the ailerons operate in opposite directions as they respond.

Rolls are simply turning the aircraft 360 degrees along the line of flight, and it flies for a few moments in inverted flight before rolling over to normal flight position. The roll can be a smooth and complete 360-degree transition or it can be a snap roll, in which you first flip the aircraft 90 degrees to fly with one wing up and the other one down and then snapped to inverted flight. Next you flip another 90 degrees to fly with opposite wing up and finally snap back to horizontal flight. This is also referred to as a four-point roll.

IMMELMANN TURNS

An Immelmann turn is a perfect diving half loop, but with the aircraft rolling 180 degrees to finish with aircraft in the normal flight attitude and heading in the opposite direction it began the maneuver. Begin the maneuver by heading into the wind so it will help lift the model through the half-loop. Most flyers allow the model to complete the half loop as an inside loop (with wing top facing inside the loop) to fly inverted for a few feet, and then apply aileron control to roll the aircraft back to level flight as it reaches the top of the loop. Advanced flyers roll the aircraft at the beginning of the loop to make the climbing loop and outside loop (with bottom of the aircraft facing inside the loop). The experts sometimes are able include the roll concurrently with climbing loop, but you need to be a true master at the controls to accomplish a combined half-loop and roll.

SPLIT-S TURNS

In the split-S, a variation of the Immelmann turn, the aircraft starts high and then dives down through a half-loop. Begin this one with aircraft heading with the wind. Most flyers make a roll while the aircraft is at the top of the loop in order to begin the half-loop with aircraft flying inverted. This allows the half roll to be half of an inside loop. The aircraft finishes the roll in the normal flying position and heading into the wind. Again, the maneuver is more difficult if the aircraft is inverted at the start to make the half-roll a half of an outside loop. The pros combine the roll and the half loop into a single seamless maneuver.

AEROBATIC COMPETITION

Once you have mastered the techniques of flying a radio control electric-powered aircraft, you may want to compare your skills with others. The premiere event for electric aircraft is the Northeast Electric Aircraft Technology (NEAT) Fair (www.neatfair.org/), which is held each summer in the Catskill Mountains of southern New York. This is an outdoor event, but there is usually a complimentary indoor event hosted by the Silent Electric Flyers of Long Island (www.sefli.org) just a few miles up the road where the flyers gather after the sun sets. The NEAT Fair is currently the largest electric model aircraft meet in North America and features dozens of suppliers, clinics, and head-to-head competition.

The AMA and other organizations sponsor pattern flying competitions for precision aerobatics. Competition is just developing through AMA for electric-powered aircraft, but specific events are constantly being added to the AMA's rulebook.

Flight Path

 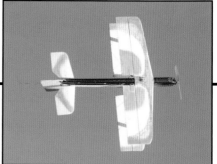

THE ROLL
The aircraft is rotated around its flight path from normal level flight to inverted flight and back around to normal level flight. The aircraft in these photos is a Northeast Sailplane 2Cool with a modified elevator and a custom paint job by Frank Dilatusch.

Flight Path

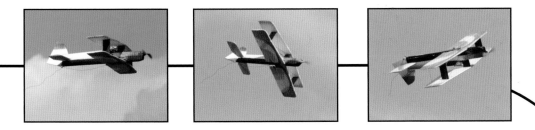

THE IMMLEMANN TURN
This maneuver begins with a 180-degree roll to inverted flight, followed immediately with a dive that is maintained for a full half-circle so the aircraft ends in normal level flight, but is heading in the opposite direction.

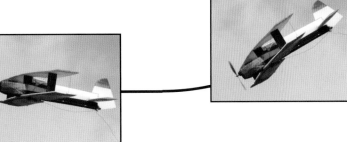

AEROBATIC IMPACT WITH SMOKE

Any aerobatic maneuver appears more spectacular if the aircraft's path lingers as a line of smoke. The TME Smart Smoker pump is a simple oil-burning system that generates the clouds of smoke that make larger aerobatic aircraft so breathtaking.

PYLON RACING

The Academy of Model Aeronautics (AMA) has national competitions and rules for virtually every type of aircraft flying competition. Most of the events are set up for fuel-powered aircraft, but flyers of electric-powered models use similar rules and set up their own events. The very quickest aircraft compete in pylon races, which are essentially races for four planes that go around a triangular course with two 300-foot legs and one 60-foot leg for

Class B models, and a triangular course with two 478-foot legs and one 100-foot leg for the more powerful Class A models. The AMA rulebook defines the classes for its sponsored electric-powered aircraft competition. One of the quicker electric-powered combinations is the relatively small Esprit Sokol with a Hacker Competition Carbon motor and a 1,300-mAh 3-cell Li-Poly battery, like Jorge Castorena's model.

COMBAT

Combat is a relatively new competition category for electric-powered aircraft, but it is a long-standing form of competition for fuel-powered model airplanes. These events simulate World War II dogfights. The AMA has a set of rules that prescribe the method for staging combat competition. Typically, four aircraft fly at once in each of four

Josh Galvin is holding his E-Flite Tribute profile airplane in a 3-D hovering maneuver with the aircraft "hanging" on the propeller.

rounds. Essentially, the pilots have 90 seconds to get airborne and the combat goes on for five minutes. Each aircraft carries a 1-inch-wide, 30-foot-long paper streamer. The object of the competition is cut the other aircrafts' streamers with your aircraft's propeller. The aircraft that lands with longest streamer wins that round. You can establish your own combat events with two or more aircraft. The most successful combat aircraft are aerobatic aircraft with quick motors and props, but you could just as easily specify that each combatant has to fly scale World War II aircraft, like the series from GWS.

An alternate method of combat is to equip each aircraft with a sonic transmitter and receiver, like the Parkzone Sonic Combat units. They are about the size of a book of matches and can be attached to top of the fuselage with Velcro. The combatants aim their aircraft at the opposing aircraft and push a switch on the transmitter that commands the Sonic Combat unit to emit a signal. If that signal hits the other aircraft, it emits a loud whine and the "hit" aircraft's motor power is cut for 10 seconds, but its other controls are untouched. If that aircraft is hit again and again, it can literally be forced to land. Conversely, "shooting" reduces power so you must conserve the number of rounds or rockets you fire. The range is about 70 feet, but obviously the closer the two aircraft are, the better the chance of a hit. The Sonic Combat units can be fitted to any X-Port equipped HobbyZone airplane, like the Firebird Commander, Aerobird Challenger, and Aerobird Xtreme or the ParkZone F-27 Stryker and Slo-V. The combat is more interesting when the combating aircraft are nearly identical in performance.

With practiced rudder, elevator, and aileron changes, Josh Galvin is able to "walk" his aircraft sideways down the field.

Jorge Castorena has upgraded his Esprit Sokol so it is quick enough be a competitive pylon racer.

3-D AND 4-D
AIRCRAFT FLIGHT MANEUVERS

Radio control model aircraft pilots have gone beyond what is possible in real aircraft with 3-D and 4-D maneuvers. A model aircraft has a bit of an advantage, as compared to a real aircraft, because the air is much thicker proportionally to the model. Your model aircraft is a fraction of the size of the real aircraft, but the air molecules that help hold your aircraft aloft are not scaled down to match the model. Thus, it is a lot easier for your model to fly than if it were a full-size aircraft. That partially explains why model airplanes and model helicopters can perform 3-D maneuvers.

About a decade ago, model aircraft pilots discovered that they could actually hang some of their aerobatic airplanes on the propeller, much like a helicopter hangs on its rotor blades. They also discovered it was possible to fly many aerobatic maneuvers with the airplane on its side, with one wing tip pointing up and the other down. These maneuvers were dubbed 3-D.

Recently, a few fliers have installed variable-pitch propellers on conventional aerobatic model airplanes. The variable-pitch propellers allow the models to hover with the propeller down and the tail up, which has been labeled 4-D flight. They also permit even more fantastic aerobatic maneuvers to be invented by model aircraft pilots with advanced skills.

HOVERING AN AIRPLANE

"Hanging on the prop" is one of the basic 3-D maneuvers. The aircraft is literally hanging from the force of the propeller, and the ailerons are used to counteract the torque from the propeller to keep the model stable. The aircraft enters the hover mode usually from a very tight half-outside loop, flying so slow that the aircraft is just beginning to climb and is on the verge of stalling and falling backwards. Knowing that, you would be wise to learn to hover with 100 feet of altitude to give yourself time to catch the model if it does stall and fall backward.

For slow speed 3-D maneuvers, you may need to fit a propeller with less pitch. The best 3-D models are the stunt aircraft designed for conventional aerobatics. These models may fly at 30 to 50 miles an hour and be able to climb vertically at a slightly less

Jorge Castorena's upgraded Northeast Sailplanes Extra 3-D and Frank Dilatusch's 2Cool profile aircraft could do combat competition—all they really need is about 30 feet of ribbon trailing behind. The aircraft have the power and maneuverability needed for combat.

Aircraft used for combat competition are some of the fastest and most maneuverable models. A 30-foot streamer trails behind this model as it heads into combat with three other similar aircraft.

Two combat aircraft dive and loop like two hawks battling in the sky. These two are fuel-powered, but today's electric-powered models have plenty of power and duration for combat.

speed. But for hovering performance, more power and less speed is needed. For example, if the model has a 9x4 propeller (9-inch diameter, 4-inch thrust), you should try a 9x6 or a 10x7 prop to achieve better control when hovering. You don't want to lose all the speed, so you may need to compromise between complete control and speed.

You need to learn to control the throttle with precision because that is the primary control that affects the model's performance when hovering. The rudder is used to help balance the model against the torque of the propeller, which is why you see models hanging from the prop with the tail slightly to the side rather than directly below the propeller. The ailerons are used to keep the model from spinning on the motor's axis through the fuselage. If your transmitter has adjustments for the throttle curve, use them to soften the throttle response for better control when hovering. Most aircraft will require just a bit of right rudder and touch of up elevator. If your transmitter has a computer, you may want to program a hover set of values so you can keep the control sticks near the center for more predictable control. As always with radio control aircraft, the controls are reversed if the model is coming toward you. Learn to hover by looking at the top of the wings before you try it with the belly facing you.

KNIFE-EDGE FLIGHT

The basic knife-edge maneuver is a quarter of a snap roll with the aircraft flying one wing up and other down so the wings are 90 degrees (or at a right angle) to the ground. In 3-D flying, the knife-edge maneuver can be continued into a loop with the rudder controlling the size of the loop, and the elevator and ailerons provide stability to maintain the knife-edge attitude. Knife-edge maneuvers are not possible with many aircraft, and they are in the advanced school of aerobatics.

Like most 3-D maneuvers, the knife-edge flight is something that cannot be accomplished with a real aircraft, but it is possible to master with a model airplane once you have developed the skills and reflex movements for conventional flight. With knife-edge flight, the fuselage and rudder provide most of the lift. The wings and stabilizer act like the rudder to help keep the aircraft on the desired trajectory.

Understand that not all model aircraft can successfully fly in the knife-edge position. Generally, aircraft that cannot generate lift from the shape of the sides of the fuselage are almost impossible to fly on their side. Surprisingly, many of the models with perfectly flat profile fuselages (typically die-cut from 1/4-inch-thick foam sheet) can be flown successfully through knife-edge maneuvers. Other aspects of the model's design can affect the model's knife-edge performance. Some airplanes, for example, are strongly affected by rudder movements and the airplane will change its attitude on the pitch (nose up or down) and roll axis automatically when the rudder is moved. These aircraft will require deft changes in elevator input to keep the aircraft on its desired flight path. With the more expensive radio transmitters, you can usually program automatic adjustments of the elevator to coincide with specific amounts of movement at the rudder. Those programs may need to be modified or overrun to adjust the aircraft in-flight for knife-edge flying.

In practice, few aircraft will fly sideways or knife-edge with the fuselage parallel to the ground. On most aircraft, the nose is somewhat higher than the tail, which is, in part, a result of the fuselage acting like an airfoil. The nose-up attitude is dictated by the relative position of the wing along the fuselage and the center of gravity of the model.

If you are flying for an audience, either just for fun or in an organized competition, you will probably want the model to fly with a cockpit, rather than landing gear facing you and your audience. You will then need to learn how to fly the model with either the wing tip up through knife-edge maneuvers. The process of learning to fly knife-edge in either direction is somewhat like learning to control the plane whether it is coming toward you or flying away from you in conventional flight. To initiate knife-edge flight, the ailerons must be moved to rotate the aircraft either right or left exactly 90 degrees. Once the aircraft is flying knife-edge, you must control its upward or downward path by moving the rudder. The rudder direction will be opposite of the direction you rolled the aircraft into the knife edge. When you rolled left, the rudder must be moved left to keep the nose up and the aircraft leveled, and vice versa.

Just to complicate things a bit further, if you make the transition from conventional level flight to knife-edge, the stick movements will be opposite what you were using. Conversely if you change from inverted flight to knife-edge, the stick movements will be the same as they were for inverted flight.

Jorge Castorena has maneuvered his E-Flite Ultimate from a hovering position, and the aircraft now is about a fourth of the way through a tight full 360-degree knife-edge loop.

CHAPTER 9
Indoor Electric Flight

MODEL AIRPLANE enthusiasts have been flying their aircraft indoors for as long as models have been flown. A typical indoor model used to be powered by rubber bands for the obvious reason that flying a fuel-powered model is not something to do indoors. The available power for indoor flight was severely limited until electric power became an option.

Most of the small- and medium-sized helicopters, like this Pro Piccolo, can perform full 3-D maneuvers in a space as small as a gymnasium.

YES, YOU CAN FLY THAT INDOORS

The development of electric power for model aircraft has expanded the choices of models to fly indoors. The manufacturers have responded with packages complete with motor, ESC, receiver, and battery, which virtually plug into the model.

The Ultra Micro aircraft may have a wingspan of less than a foot and weigh less than 2 ounces, complete with batteries. They can fly for 15 minutes and more. The Sub Micro aircraft are a bit larger, with wingspans in the 12- to 15-inch range and a weight of less than 3 ounces.

Perhaps the most popular indoor fliers are the Micro Size models that weigh 3 to 8 ounces. There are dozens of ARF models in this class. Some have profile fuselages and wings, and some are equipped with fully formed foam fuselages and wings.

The parking lot, park flyer, and backyard flyer aircraft that weigh 8 to 14 ounces are designed to be flown outdoors. However, most of them are capable of flying slow enough to be indoor models. Model aircraft, such as the Ikarus Shock Flyer, can be flown slow enough to perform a variety of 3-D maneuvers in a space as small as a gymnasium.

There are several ready-to-fly Sub Micro model aircraft, like the $15 Cox Aero X that can be flown indoors.

The Northeast IFO-3 flying disc is less than a foot across, but it is as maneuverable as most conventional aircraft.

The small delta-wing aircraft, like the Ace Sim RC Carbon Falcon, are small enough and offer enough control at slow speeds to be flown indoors.

Any electric-powered radio control helicopter can be flown indoors if the pilot has enough experience. Practically speaking, the smaller choppers like Hirobo's Sky Robo Mini RC from MRC, the Ikarus Piccolo series, Kyosho's Caliber replica of the Schweizer 300C, and others will fly as readily indoors as outdoors.

THE INDOOR FLYING FIELD

Indoor flight introduces both new challenges and freedoms. There is the obvious challenge of hitting the ceiling or the walls, but that soon becomes a simple boundary to avoid. There is no likely chance for wind shift or for the wind to blow at higher speeds anywhere in the room. Having stated that, keep an eye out for what happens if someone does open one of the outside doors—gusts are not impossible occurrences indoors.

Indoor flight competitions have been held in ballrooms with 12-foot-plus ceilings. That's a challenge. Try to find a really large gym, a university fieldhouse, an empty aircraft hangar, or a large industrial structure. Sometimes a local Realtor can help locate both a site and an owner. Never consider flying at a site where you do not have written permission to use it from the owners.

The Hirobo Sky Robo Mini RC is ready to fly and has counter-rotating rotors for really easy control and stability indoors or out.

The GWS Dragonfly is ready-to-fly right out of the box.

SUB MICRO FLYERS

There are some great choices of realistic aircraft in this class, including a series of foam models of World War II aircraft from Dynamics Unlimited and DJ Aerotech. There is also a similar series of laser-cut foam aircraft.

ULTRA MICRO FLYERS

There are a number of die-cut and laser-cut foam profile toy fliers that fall into this tiny class of indoor aircraft. However, this class is the preference of many model builders because it provides an opportunity to create some truly unique models. These models weigh 2 ounces or less, so they are extremely delicate. Indoor Model Supply has several kits, and there are some ultralight motor, ESC, transmitter, and battery packages from FMA Direct and Dynamic Web Enterprises.

RUBBER-POWERED CONVERSIONS

If you have the skill and interest to build tissue-covered stick models with rubber power, you can probably convert these kits to electric power. The electric power will require modifications during the assembly stage, but a skilled modeler can often retro-fit electric motors to an existing aircraft. Some of the newer kits from firms such as Peck Polymers and Indoor Model Supply include suggestions for adapting electric power. You will need the lightest available motor, ESC, transmitter, and battery package.

INDOOR FLYING

Electric-powered model airplanes that weigh less than 8 ounces are usually slow and responsive enough to be flown in area as small as a basketball court. The tiny 2- to 4-ounce planes are sometimes controllable enough to be flown in your living room. You will discover that an indoor area, even a large gymnasium, is much smaller than the nearly limitless outdoor parks. You will be more comfortable flying indoors if you select a model that can fly at relatively slow speeds. Models that have deeply chambered wing airfoils (where the underside of the wing is concave) can help to provide more control for slower flights. Experienced indoor flyers suggest that the model is small enough if it has a wing loading of less than 5 ounces per square foot, a measurement derived by dividing the square foot area of the wing by the model's total weight.

The Ikarus Pro Piccolo is an upgraded standard Piccolo with 3-D flight capability.

Some of the least expensive profile models, like this Ikarus Shock-Flyer YAK 54, can perform the most complex 3-D flights indoors when fitted with more powerful brushless motors and low-speed propellers.

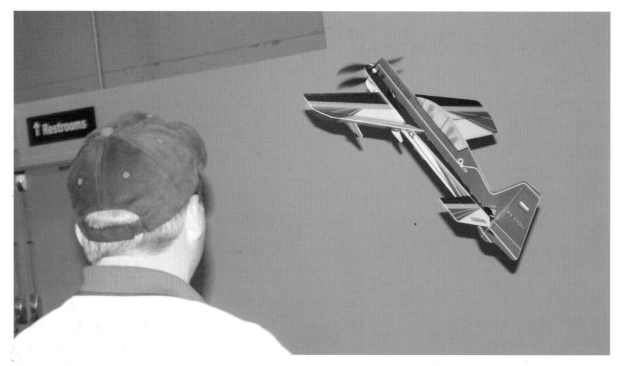

Andrew Jersky pulls his Ikarus Shock Flyer YAK 54 into a 3-D hover maneuver inside a convention center.

These profile models can be flown at a walking pace, which makes landings relatively simple to accomplish.

The profile models, like the Shock-Flyer YAK 54, can also perform knife-edge maneuvers. This one is flying from right to left at this angle.

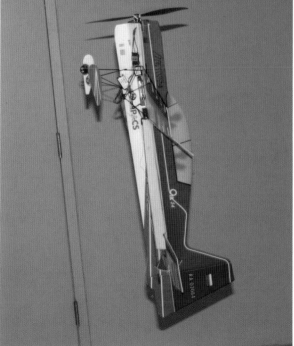

The Ikarus Shock-Flyer YAK 54 hangs from the prop in a hovering 3-D maneuver.

CHAPTER 10
Silent Helicopters

THE ELECTRIC POWER revolution within the model aircraft hobby has had the most effect on model helicopters. One of the advantages of a helicopter, real or miniature, is that it can be flown just about anywhere. With fuel-powered models, the gas fumes and noise caused flying sites to be well removed from civilization. With electric power, you can fly a small helicopter in your living room and the largest can be flown in your backyard.

This Heli-Quick EP-10 is fitted with a Hacker C50-15L motor.

HELICOPTER FLIGHT BY RADIO CONTROL

The more expensive radio-controlled model helicopters have rotor blade controls that include variable pitch. That control allows the helicopter to have far more precise control than speeding up the rotation of the rotors. If the variable pitch can range through about 90 degrees, the rotor can be reversed so that it pushes the helicopter down rather than pulling it up. Why would you want to push it up? To fly upside down, of course. The variable-pitch rotors have allowed model helicopter pilots to perform aerobatic feats, including flying the helicopter upside down. Real helicopters do not have that capability. With the best variable-pitch rotors, model helicopters can perform loops and rolls and combinations of these maneuvers to duplicate just about any aerobatic pattern a conventional model airplane can complete.

FLYING A CHOPPER

Helicopters are far more difficult to learn to fly than a conventional airplane. One of the differences between the two types of aircraft is that the rotor blades on the helicopter serve several flight functions at once. The rotors act as the wings for the helicopter and provide forward motion (when tilted forward slightly), pitch (nose up or down), roll or lean (when the rotor tilts to one side or the other), altitude controland right left turn control.

Virtually all of the control for a helicopter is accomplished by the larger rotor blades. The small tail-rotor is used primarily for stability, and on the larger models, it helps turn the aircraft and trim the aircraft to a precise course. The main rotor blades are mounted on a fully articulated universal joint called a swash plate. In addition to the universal joint, the more advanced helicopters have a controllable pitch for the rotor blades. All this control is accomplished while the rotor is spinning away.

Stan Michalski practices his flying technique with his Heli-Quick EP-10 at the 2004 NEAT Fair.

It's best for beginners to launch a helicopter by hand, but you will need an assistant to operate the transmitter or know how to work the throttle with your left thumb.

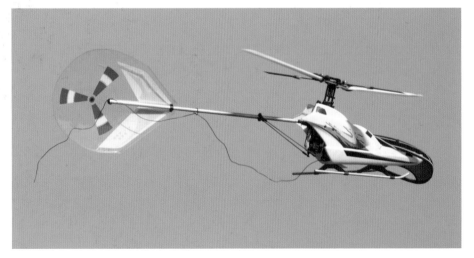

The tail rotor is a clear plastic fin painted to look like a rotor on this older Kyosho Hyperflight helicopter. Jim Cloud upgraded it with three-channel control for the rotor and motor.

Thick grass is one of the best places to learn to fly a helicopter because it can cushion the landings.

CONTROL FOR A MODEL HELICOPTER

The swash plate below the rotor blades is connected to three servo motors, which push and pull at specific areas of the swash plate to provide the precise degree of tilt needed for pitch, aileron (tilt), and elevator control. A fourth servo controls the rudder (turn). Motor speed control is usually carried out by a fifth channel operating an ESC as with conventional airplanes.

The radio control transmitter for the more advanced helicopter models has control for the rotor speed on the left stick (forward for more speed or to gain altitude, back for less speed or to lose altitude). Moving the right stick left leans the helicopter to the right and moves it slightly to the right and the opposite occurs when moving the left stick. The right stick provides elevator control by altering the tilt on the rotor so that moving the control stick forward pushes the nose down. Moving the stick back pulls the nose up. The left stick is also used for rudder control (moving the rotor) to turn the helicopter right by moving the stick right and vice versa.

Ikarus offers a Training Carriage with foam balls at each corner to make landings less of a shock to the model.

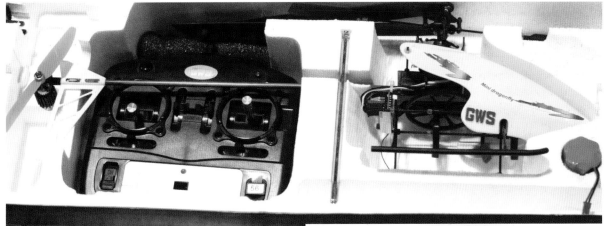

The GWS Dragonfly is ready-to-fly right out of the box. The package includes a matching transmitter.

The rotor head on the GWS Dragonfly is fitted with ball bearings. This one has the optional freewheel (the large geared wheel) and the EHS-100 green-anodized aluminum heat sink for the motor.

STABILITY BY GYRO

The helicopters usually have an electronic gyro in the control circuit. The gyro automatically adjusts the rotor's position to counteract the rotor's torque, which tries to swing the helicopter to the side. The faster the rotor turns, the more the helicopter wants to turn. The gyro detects any movement of the nose of the helicopter and automatically adjusts the controls to keep the nose pointed straight, regardless of rotor speed. The more advanced gyros adjust the tail-rotor to keep the helicopter on the correct course.

The ARF and ready-to-fly helicopters usually include a gyro. The gyro can, however, be upgraded to provide the faster response, which you may need for 3-D aerobatics. The Ikarus Trio-Gyro is typical of the best gyros in offering stabilizing control for all three axis.

MORE PERFORMANCE
THAN A REAL HELICOPTER

All of the electric-powered radio control helicopters, even the lower priced ready-to-fly models, will duplicate the performance of real helicopters, including turns, hovering, and reverse movement. Models with brushless motors and Li-Poly batteries can fly for as long as 30 minutes, but most are limited from 5 to 15 minutes because the motors can get extremely hot. GWS and others offer aluminum heat sinks that can be fitted around the motor to improve its cooling capacity.

The Hirobo Sky Robo Mini RC (see Chapter 9) is unusual because it has two sets of rotor blades that rotate in opposite directions. The counter-rotating (XRB) design provides far more stability than a conventional single-direction rotor. The blades are made of special flexible foam to avoid damaging anything they hit and are flexible enough that they will flex instead of break. Interactive Concepts' Blade Runner is another entry-level helicopter with counter-rotating rotors. Both of these models offer a truly stable flight and are recommended for those who want to learn how much fun it is to fly a helicopter the easy way.

The more expensive helicopters can perform maneuvers that are not possible with a real helicopter, including flying upside down and performing loops and combinations of patterns. It takes practice to learn the control inputs needed to accomplish these maneuvers.

There are several flight simulator programs, including the EasySIM from the Ikarus Piccolo series of helicopters, and they can make it much easier to learn to fly a model helicopter. You can learn to fly a model helicopter on a flight simulator and then apply that experience to the actual model.

The Ikarus Piccolo Pro is a relatively small helicopter, but it has full 3-D capability so you can fly it upside down once you develop the skill.

Most of the model helicopters have a simple vacuum-formed cowl to cover the machinery. Ikarus offers several replicas of real helicopter bodies for the Ikarus Piccolo Pro.

The key to flying inverted with a model helicopter is a full control over rotor pitch—called collective pitch—like that on this Piccolo Pro.

FLYING YOUR HELICOPTER

One of the advantages of flying a helicopter is that you can learn with aircraft heading away from you. Develop the reflexes you need to land, takeoff, and move right and left and up and down by watching from the rear of the helicopter. When you turn the helicopter around so it is flying toward you, the inputs from the transmitter levers must be reversed, just as they are with a conventional airplane. You can use the techniques suggested in Chapter 5 for learning to overcome the right-at-you disorientation suggested for conventional aircraft.

To land a helicopter, you must gently let off on the speed control. You cannot shut off the power and hope to glide to a landing as you might with some airplanes. Shut off the power with a helicopter and it will fall like a stone. Practice landings at the same sessions when you practice takeoffs. During the takeoff, allow the helicopter to rise just a few feet, then back off the throttle and land the model. With minimal altitude, a crash is not likely to do too much damage. Some of the helicopter makers offer an auto-rotation flywheel that can be fitted to aircraft to keep the rotors moving even without power. Ikarus has them for its Piccolo, Eco 7, and Eco 8 series, and some are available from other manufacturers.

For maximum control, especially for 3-D flying maneuvers, a powered tail rotor is a must. Larger models may have twin tail-rotors, each with its own motor.

COMPUTERIZED TRANSMITTER CONTROL

With simple helicopter flying maneuvers, you will be able to maintain control by moving the sticks on the transmitter. The control gets a bit trickier when the aircraft is moving toward you, and you need some real dexterity when you progress to 3-D flights, where the helicopter performs loops, rolls, and inverted flight. The top-of-the-line transmitters include computer programming. You will be able to program the specific fine-tuning adjustments that work best with each helicopter and program combinations of control adjustments. The transmitter will also make some of the minor in-flight adjustments automatically so that you can concentrate just on maneuvering the model.

CRASH CONTROL

If you are learning with smaller helicopters, you may want to buy one of the training undercarriage landing gear units with foam balls on the extreme ends of spring-wire landing gear. Ikarus has one for its small Piccolo series that can be adapted to other helicopter models. Ikarus also has lightweight version with carbon fiber rods in place of the piano wires.

MODEL HELICOPTER CHOICES

There are now several entry-level radio control helicopters that sell for under $400, including the radio transmitter and charger. The Hirobo Sky Robo Mini RC is ready-to-fly, and there are a number of ARF choppers including the Ikarus Eco Piccolo,

GWS Dragonfly HFD3A, Hobby Lobby's Honey Bee, Kyosho's Caliber M24 (with a replica of the Schweizer 300C body), and kits like the Lite Machine's Corona Model 120. These models are usually about 20 inches long with 20-inch rotors.

Some of the smaller helicopters, including the Corona, can be upgraded with a Choppahedz collective pitch kit, and the Piccolo can be upgraded with an Ikarus conversion set (you will also need a four-channel transmitter and receiver), as well as a direct tail-drive tail-rotor to perform 3-D aerobatics. The Ikarus Pro Piccolo with brushless motor, ESC, and servos (no batteries, receiver, or transmitter included) is under $800.

The larger electric-powered helicopters are 3 to 4 feet long with 4-foot rotors. The Ikarus Eco 7 has a 37-inch rotor, the Eco 8 has a 41-inch rotor, and the Eco 17 has a 47-inch rotor. The Mikado Logo 20 has a 48-inch rotor. The larger helicopters can run to $1,000 and more.

The majority of the electric-powered helicopters are generic designs based on a composite of typical real helicopter design features. Some of the models, however, are replicas of the more famous helicopters. Ikarus offers replacement bodies to duplicate the shapes of the Bell 222 Airwolf, Hughes 300, and Bell UH1-D Huey.

SOME HELICOPTER SETUPS

- Smartech Aero Hawk with Like 90 rotors and carbon fiber motor mount and head stiffeners, A Johnson 250 motor with GWS heat sink and dual tail motors.

- Lite Machines Corona with Astro Flight brushless 020 motor and the special Corona installation kit with ESC and your choice of 2100-mAh Li-Poly battery pack.

- Ikarus Piccolo Pro with a Piccoboard Pro/ESC, three Lexors micro 100 servos, and a 720-mAh Li-Poly battery.

- Mikado Logo 20 with a Hacker C50-15XL Brushless motor, Castle Creations Phoenix-80 controller, four Hitec HS605BB servos, Futaba 1024 PCM receiver, and a 401 gyro.

The Ikarus Eco 7 is a medium-sized model that is available ready-to-fly. All you need to do is plug in the battery pack and fly.

CHAPTER 11
Maintenance & Repair

TODAY'S ELECTRIC-POWERED model aircraft are incredibly reliable and strong enough to withstand some horrendous crashes. Like any machine, they require some maintenance, and if you crash them often enough, they will need some repairs. You can also upgrade your model for more reliable performance and better resistance to crashes. And you can custom paint your ARF, or perhaps you may try your hand at building your own aircraft from kits or plans.

Josh Glavin attached some 1/16-inch carbon fiber rods to bottom of the wings of his E-Flite Ultimate to improve the model's stability and crash resistance.

BULLETPROOF YOUR AIRCRAFT MODELS

Eventually you are going to crash your model. Even the very best and most experienced flyers push their limits and lose control. There is always that unpredictable wind gust or an attack by an out-of-control model aircraft. There are several things you can do with your models to make them less likely to disintegrate in a crash.

The electric-powered models are generally much lighter than fuel-powered models. Part of the success of a long duration and superb performance has been the light weight of electric-powered models. The lighter weight makes the chances of the model crashing less likely. The foam models have the built-in shock absorbing capacity, which foam provides.

When you mount the heavier components—such as the motor and batteries—isolate them with rubber cushioning in case of sudden deceleration in a crash. The motor and battery pack can be held in place with rubber bands. The rubber bands will give a bit in a crash, perhaps enough to prevent the motor or battery pack from tearing loose. Use double-stick foam tape to mount the servos and receivers so the foam takes some of the shock for them.

CRASH-PROOFING WITH CARBON FIBER

The larger profile ARF and kit models are often reinforced with strips of carbon fiber (a modification you can also make), running the length of each wing from tip to near the wing mount in the fuselage. Additional strips run from the motor mount to the tail and near the leading edge of the wing from wing tip to wing tip. Midwest Products offers a range of carbon fiber strips in lengths up to 3 feet that are available through hobby dealers and some hardware stores.

Wing tips and hinge edges can be reinforced with carbon fiber rods taped to the model with clear packing tape to the model. You can protect the fuselage with a single layer of clear packing tape. Attaching tape to protect the wings would add too much weight, but the wing's leading edge can be protected with carbon rods and a 3/4-inch strip of clear packing tape.

Andrew Jersky carries some tubes of foam-safe cyanoacrylate (CA) cement and clear tape in his pockets to make quick field repairs of any minor damage.

Before: Eddie Truillo's Clever Boy takes its maiden flight with an experienced flyer at the controls.

THE TAKE-ALONG TOOL KIT

When you head for the flying site, you will want to take a few items in addition to the aircraft and radio control transmitter. The model(s) should be checked over at home for any potential operating problems. You will undoubtedly need to make some repairs at the flying field, if only to recharge the batteries.

Buy a battery charger with an adaptor to plug into a car's cigarette lighter so you can use the charger at the flying site. If you buy a second battery pack, you can use it to replace the pack in the aircraft and the first pack can be charging while you fly with the second. You can then fly almost continuously for as long as you wish and stop only to change battery packs. The smaller battery packs can recharge in as little as 20 minutes, but the larger packs can take an hour. However, you can fly for about that same amount of time, especially when you add in the launch, landing, and battery changing time to the cycle.

The most valuable item in my take-along tool kit is a hot glue gun with an adaptor for my cigarette lighter. Camping and travel trailer shops sell 110-volt converters that will plug into your cigarette lighter. A lighter weight alternative would be to use the foam-safe cyanoacrylate cements (CA) like PK Industries' NI-1000E foam-safe CA and matching spray-on QT IV activator.

I also carry a roll of 1 1/2-inch-wide clear packing tape for quick repairs, like taping down a loose receiver. A wide selection of rubber bands is useful for holding down battery packs or to replace rubber bands that hold down the wings. I take a pair of small needle-nose pliers and diagonal cutters with a few lengths of piano wire to replace any broken servo connectors. I include any tools I may have used to assemble the model, including both plain and Phillips-head screwdrivers, any special screwdriver bits, and Allen wrenches. I also have a few spare control horns to replace broken parts, which can be attached with hot glue.

The most essential take-along spares are replacement propellers. I usually have at least four with pitches to match what has proven best for each aircraft. I also take two or three alternative pitches for occasions where a different propeller can make it easier to fly. I carry three spare mounting nuts with the appropriate wrench and also have a half-dozen replacement motor-mounting screws and nuts. A bottle of all-purpose cleanser, paper towels, and alcohol-soaked wipes can keep the messes to a minimum. If your radio transmitter has plug-in frequency crystal sets, buy two or three extra sets with different frequencies (in matched sets of TX for the transmitter and RX for the receiver) so you have a choice when you get to flying field.

Hobby shops sell special toolboxes for model aircraft that have a twin-yoke bracket on the top with padded arms to support the model while you work on it. Bring a 2x4-foot towel or rug to provide a work space and something to catch any dropped parts so you won't spend hours searching in the grass.

REPAIRING CRASHES AT THE SITE

You can often repair any crashes right at the flying site if you bring along a few tools and supplies. Most of the super glue cements (CA) cure with self-generated heat and are not suitable for foam aircraft components. However, there are some newer CA cements, such as PK Industries NI-1000E foam-safe CA and matching QT IV activator (accelerator—for instant cure) that are designed to be used specifically with foam. The foam-safe CA will also work with balsa and other materials. A 5-minute epoxy can also be useful for repairing really bad breaks.

If a foam model has crashed badly enough to tear off a wing and rip out the battery, you should reinforce any repairs. You can use common bamboo skewers or buy a couple of 2-foot pieces of 1/16-inch carbon fiber rod for less than $5 to use for reinforcement. Cut a few pieces of rod about 2 to 3 inches long to use for emergency repairs. You will probably not be able measure the amount of weight the carbon fiber rod and CA cement will add to the model.

After: This is Eddie Truillo's Clever Boy after a major mid-air collision because the flyers were both on the same radio frequency. Balsa models that are this splintered can seldom be repaired, even with super glue and patience.

Ron Evans rebuilt a model of the HalAir kit of the Glassair sailplane and converted it from fuel power to electric power. It now has an Acro-brand Outrunner motor, a folding propeller, and an 8-cell NiMH battery pack.

A typical crash may result in half of the stabilizer being broken away from the fuselage of a foam model. If a covered balsa model crashes, similar damage may result and you may be able to use this same technique with balsa.

Test-fit the broken part to see precisely how it should be aligned if your repair is 100 percent successful. Take a 2-inch piece of carbon fiber rod (or bamboo skewer) and coat all but a half-inch of the rod with foam-safe CA. Push the CA-coated carbon fiber rod down the center of the stabilizer from the broken end. Then spread a thin bead of CA along the protruding half-inch of rod. Apply a thin bead of the foam-safe CA to the two broken faces. Look down the fuselage to see how the stabilizer is supposed to fit, and then carefully push the stabilizer into its precise original position as the exposed rod pushes its way into the fuselage. Run a thin bead of the foam-safe CA around the broken seam. Use a toothpick or short piece of steel piano wire to apply a thin bead of

the activator along the seam to set the CA on the surface instantly. It's wise to wait an hour to allow the CA a bit of time to set before flying the model.

If the battery bracket or motor mount have torn loose, you may need to reinforce the carbon pin repair with a small piece of fiberglass cloth. PKL offers a 5-minute-cure two-part epoxy that can be used at home or in the field.

I have also had success with the hot glues that are designed for use with foam. You may even be able to find a hot glue gun (with matching glue sticks for use with foam) that can be adapted to use in a cigarette lighter socket. The hot glues are tricky to use because they harden almost instantly. Thus the parts must be fitted together, separated while the glue is squirted in, and pushed back into place while the glue is still hot. You can use the same glue for wood- and vinyl-covered models. The hot glue can also be used to secure battery-pack mounting brackets and to secure loosened servos.

Ron Evans used flush-fitting covers in the fuselage. Magnetic catches make it easy to change or charge the battery pack.

IMPROVED CONTROL SURFACE HINGES

The rudder flap, elevators, and ailerons on many models are hinged with a single piece of mylar tape. In time, the tape can become loose or begin to tear, so the control flap no longer operates with precision and causes possible loss of control. If the tape is loose, you may be able to pull it free. On foam models, the tape's grip is usually stronger than the foam so you'll tear into the model if you attempt to remove the tape. Use a razor blade to trim the tape right to loosened edges, freeing the control surface. Now you can apply a fresh strip of tape. You can buy mylar tape at some hobby shops, but the packing tape with fiberglass reinforcing strands are tougher and will usually last longer than mylar. A width of 3/4 inch is usually wide enough, but 1 1/2-inch fiber-reinforced packaging tape is also available. Before you apply the tape, place a 0.06-inch carbon fiber rod (from Midwest Products) along the edges of the control surface and the rudder, elevator, or wing to reinforce the area and keep it straight.

UPGRADED LANDING GEAR

Most model aircraft that have landing gear use a bent piano wire bracket to mount the wheels to the fuselage. If the wire begins to tear loose, you can usually secure it with hot glue designed for use with foam.

Most hobby shops offer lightweight foam tires and wheels that can be used to replace the stiff plastic wheels supplied with most model aircraft. The foam wheels usually have bearings to match the steel piano wire on the model. If this isn't the case, then the shop may have reducing bushings or brass tubing that can be cut (with a razor saw) to fit the wheels. Secure the wheels with a piece of tiny fuel tube held firmly with a drop of CA.

The hinges for the rudder and elevator are thin strips of aluminum wrapped around aluminum tubes for the hinge pins.

The GWS Spitfire is fully decorated, but the foam still shows through the paint.

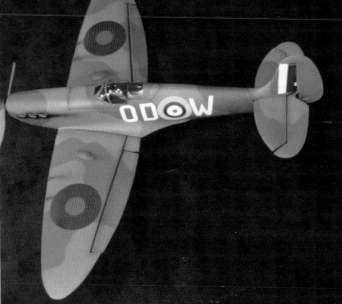

Here is GWS Spitfire repainted with Pactra's R/C acrylic paint and decorated with Microscale decals.

Steven Stratt's superb built-from-scratch replica of the Fokker D.VIII has a Williams Brothers pilot figure.

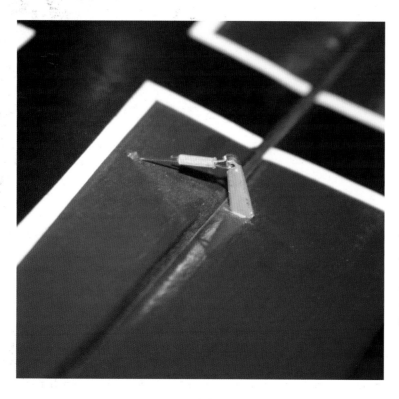

The horns that control the ailerons on Steven Stratt's Fokker D.VIII were shaped from 0.040-inch aluminum sheet to be as small as possible and still provide complete control.

BATTERY TIE-DOWNS

Many of the ARF and simple kit models include a compartment or bracket to mount a battery pack. Sometimes hooks are provided so that rubber bands can be used to hold the battery. The rubber bands are a good idea because they can help absorb some of the shock of landing, preventing the battery pack from tearing loose. On some models, you may want to move the battery pack forward and backward a bit to adjust the model's center of gravity. You can combine the best of both worlds by using a strip of Velcro on the battery pack and the bracket that holds the battery pack. For a bit of extra cushion, use a layer of double-stick foam tape between the Velcro and the battery pack.

HATCH LATCHES

Even with foam models, there is usually a cover to hide the receiver and battery pack. There may be other covers for access to the motor and/or the servos. You can retain these hatches with a simple 1/4-inch-diameter steel washer and a lightweight rare earth magnet from an electronic store. Apply epoxy or hot glue to affix the magnet to the hatch or cover and attach the steel washer to the aircraft so the magnet and washer touch to hold the cover or hatch in place.

Chuck Shafer used Testors paint pens to simulate the bullet holes in his GWS Spitfire. The holes hide a broken fuselage that was repaired (successfully) with PK Industries NI-1000E foam-safe CA cement.

CUSTOM PAINT AND MARKING

Most of the aircraft models are painted and decorated. The bare foam edges of the profile models can be colored with a felt tip pen. There's no reason why you cannot repaint your aircraft to match a different real aircraft or customize it to suit your personal taste.

A layer of paint will not add enough weight your model to affect its performance. Testors' Pactra brand offers a complete range of aerosol paints in the R/C Acrylic series that are intended for use on foam. The series includes FAA Standard, U.S. Standard, Royal Air Force, Japanese, and German military colors for both modern and Word War II–era aircraft.

Microscale and others offer decals for both commercial and military aircraft of all eras. To apply decals, cut each decal from the sheet. Dip only the decals you are going to use (on one side of the aircraft or wing) into warm water using tweezers. Submerge the decal, then immediately place it on a facial tissue for about a minute so the water has time to soak through and dissolve the glue on the back of the decal. Put a drop or two of water on the area where you will be placing the decal. Lift the decal and the paper backing with tweezers and position them on the aircraft. Slide the decal about 1/16-inch off the paper backing with the tip of a hobby knife. Grip the exposed paper backing with tweezers and pull it from beneath the decal while you hold the decal itself onto the model with a number 1-size paint brush. Position the decal exactly where you want it and wick away any excess water with the corner of a facial tissue. Let the decal dry overnight. Protect the decals with two very light coats of Testors DullCote aerosol paint.

Electric-powered models can be as realistic as you want to make them. Details cut from balsa or shaped from aluminum or carbon fiber will add little weight. Lightweight detailed pilot figures are available from Polk's and other hobby stores. Frank Galler made miniature control horns for his Fokker C.VIII (see Chapter 1).

Polk's offers a range of fully painted feather-light pilot figures in sizes to match the popular radio control aircraft.

This much-modified Carl Goldberg Mirage with custom decals was a simple fuel-to-electric power conversion.

This high-wing classic Hacker Henri Mignet Avionette was assembled from an A J Models balsa wood kit with a ply bulkhead for a sturdy motor mount.

BUILD YOUR OWN AIRCRAFT

There is still ample opportunity for those who would rather build than buy their model aircraft. I have deliberately avoided most of the kit and built-from-scratch models because there is no absolute need to build. However, for many model aircraft enthusiasts, building is almost as enjoyable as flying. There are thousands of kits for every size and type of model imaginable, and nearly all of them include the materials to allow the model to be powered by an electric motor.

Many of today's kits include pre-painted and assembled fuselages, wings, and rudders that must be decorated with decals. Sometimes, the flaps must be cut and hinged, and the servos and control rods need to be installed. There are dozens of choices, from tiny indoor models to large outdoor kits like Mountain Models P-38 with a 38-inch wingspan, Hobby Lobby's twin-motored P-38 Lightning with a 42-inch wingspan, to the Giant Scale models with an 86-inch wingspan from Kondor.

The model aircraft magazines publish plans and there are ads for dozens of sources for plans, like Hostetler's Plans and others. Ron Evans used plans to build his stick model replica of the Mohawk. For electric flight (as opposed to rubber-band power suggested for the original model), he used plywood for the bulkheads and spruce spines. He powered it with an MP Jet brushless motor and used 600-mAh NiCd batteries.

Scale models, like this built-from-scratch 40-inch wingspan stick model of the J-3 Piper Cub (from Hostetler's Plans), can fly faster and perform aerobatics that their real counterparts cannot. The model is fitted with a Hacker B20 motor and a 4:1 gearbox with a 650-mAh Li-Poly battery pack.

There is little difference between building a model to be powered by a fuel-burning engine and one to be powered by an electric motor. Most of the published plans for balsa wood models can be adapted to electric power. Experienced builders try to save as much weight as possible by substituting thinner materials and reinforcing their models with a half-dozen carbon fiber strips. You may also need to build a mount for the battery pack, but most include a place for the batteries needed for receiver power, even in a fuel-powered model. You may, however, need to move the battery pack further forward, and the pack you use for an electric-powered plane may be a much different shape than the one suggested for a fuel-powered plane.

Some modelers are resurrecting their fuel-powered airplanes and converting them to electric power. Many years ago Steven Stratt built this replica of World War I Fokker D.VIII from plans. He replaced the 0.09-ci displacement fuel-burning engine with a Hacker brushless motor and Li-Poly batteries. The model is a superb example of a true scale model. He upgraded the kit with an aluminum cowl from Tatone and built balsa machine guns and other super details.

The Mohawk is covered with semi-translucent Monokote and applied with an iron to create a taut surface.

The Mohawk has balsa wood formers with spruce spars for strength and a plywood bulkhead.

Ron Evans built this Mohawk from plans that were intended for a fuel-powered model.

Ron Evans modified the plans for his Mohawk by repositioning the forward bulkhead to accommodate an MP Jet brushless motor.

This RN Models Playboy was built from a kit designed to accept a fuel-burning engine. There are photos of the electric engine installation in Chapter 3.

This Stinson Voyager 108 was built from Hostetler's plans.

STICK MODELS

The traditional method of building an inner structure from sheet balsa bulkheads and balsa strip spars is still popular with model airplane builders. These models are often called stick models because the kit box contains a large pile of balsa sticks. Firms like Dumas, Comet, Carl Goldberg, Peck Polymers, and others still offer these kits. Today, there are hundreds of ARF and ready-to-fly models that have the wings, fuselage, rudder, and stabilizer assembled from sheets and sticks and covered with plastic sheets. The assembly work is done in China and the ARF models, like Northeast's Mamba and Aristo's giant Fokker SR.1 triplane, can be assembled in a few hours. It might take a hundred hours to build and finish a similar kit.

Ron Evans began flying powered sailplanes decades ago, and he has converted a number of his kits from fuel to electric power. He rebuilt a model of the HalAir kit of the Glassair sailplane with a new Coverite covering—in place of the original tissue paper—and from fuel power to electric power with an Acro-brand Outrunner motor, folding propeller, and an 8-cell NiMH battery pack.

Ron used an RN Models' Playboy Jr. powered sailplane kit (now out of production) that was intended for a fuel-powered engine for a fuel-to-electric conversion. He converted the kit to fit a GWS 100 electric motor during the construction. The motor is geared 6:1 and is fitted with a folding propeller. An 8-cell 300-mAh NiMH battery pack provides enough power for over an hour of soaring flight.

The traditional tissue paper covering is now only used by a few modelers building aircraft to fly indoors. Most of the kits are covered with polyester sheets from firms like Coverite, Aerokote, Pactra, Litespan, and others. Some of these coverings are pre-glued and can be attached by simply running over them with a hot iron. Most are slightly translucent so you can see the delicate structure beneath the covering. The Litespan covering offers both translucent and opaque covering and is not pre-glued. The surfaces where it will touch must be coated with cement before the covering is applied. The Litespan Balsaloc or Fix-It cement from SIG is heat activated so you can apply it to the places where the covering will touch, press the covering in place, and use an iron to heat-seal the Litespan to the model. All of these covering materials shrink with heat so the ironing process cements the covering and stretches it taut.

Kondor Models has a range of large scale model kits with fiberglass fuselages and polyurethane-covered wings, rudders, and stabilizers. Their P-38 Lightning is available in several different paint schemes.

CHAPTER 12
Clubs and Publications

PUBLICATIONS

3-D Flyer
It is about equally divided between electric- and fuel-powered aircraft, but focuses on 3-D-style aerobatic aircraft and concepts. Published by Kiona Publishing, Inc., P.O. Box 4250, West Richland, WA 99353 (www.3-DFlyer.com).

Backyard Flyer
This publication is exclusively about electric-powered aircraft. Published by Air Age Media, 100 East Ridge, Ridgefield, CT 06877 (www.airage.com).

Fly R/C Monthly
This magazine includes both electric- and fuel-powered aircraft of all types, but about 70 percent of the content is electric. Published by Maplegate Media Group, 650 Danbury Road, Ridgefield, CT 06877 (www.flyrc.com).

Model Aviation
The monthly publication of the Academy of Model Aeronautics, 5161 E. Memorial Drive, Muncie, IN 47302, (765) 287-1256, Fax: (765) 289-4248 (www.modelaircraft.org/mag/index.htm).

Quiet & Electric Flight International
This British monthly is distributed by Traplet Distribution U.S.A. Ltd., P.O. Box 350, Monticello, IL 61856 (www.qefimagazine.com/).

Quiet Flyer
Exclusively for electric-powered aircraft, this magazine is published by Kiona Publishing, Inc., P.O. Box 4250, West Richland, WA 99353 (www.quietflyer.com).

RC MicroFlight
This monthly is for primarily indoor flying models with rubber bands and free flight as well as electric power. The subscription includes a web version and is published by Air Age Media, 100 East Ridge, Ridgefield, CT 06877 (www.rcmicroflight.com).

CLUBS

Academy of Model Aeronautics (AMA), 5161 E. Memorial Drive, Muncie, IN 47302, (765) 287-1256, Fax: (765) 289-4248 (www.modelaircraft.org). The AMA is the largest flying model aircraft club in North America, and has a monthly magazine and hundreds of affiliated clubs. Most of the clubs were founded with fuel-powered aircraft models, but the majority now include groups flying electric-powered radio control aircraft.

Boston Micronauts (www.bostonmicronauts.org).

Electric Flyers Only, Inc., AMA Charter 2354, Croswell, MI 48422 (www.members.aol.com/kmyersefo/). A comprehensive list of electric radio control clubs is available.

National Indoor Remote-controlled Aircraft Council (NIRAC). Contact: Dave Robelen, Route 4 Box 369, Farmville, VA 23901 (www.nirac.org).

National Miniature Pylon Racing Association (NMPRA). Contact: Bob Brogdon, 5251 Hermitage Drive, Powder Springs, GA 30127 (http://www.nmpra.org).

National Society of Radio Controlled Aerobatics (NSRCA). Contact: Catherine Reuther, 5456 Peachtree Industrial Blvd Suite 176, Chamblee, GA 30341 (www.nsrca.org).

R/C Combat Association (RCCA). Contact: Lou Melancon, 105 Morton Walk, Alpharetta, GA 30022 (www.rccombat.com/rcca.asp).

Rocky Mountain E-Flyers. Contact Ron Evans, Rocky Mountain Electric Flyers, 1262 Elizabeth Street #204, Denver, CO 80206, (720) 220-3384, (www.rmeflyers.org/).

Silent Electric Flyers of Long Island (www.sefli.org/).

EVENTS

JR Indoor Electric Festival (www.jriefestival.com).

National Model Aviation Championships (NATS) It is the largest model airplane event in the world, mostly fuel-powered aircraft, but there are events for electric-powered aircraft. Academy of Model Aeronautics, 5161 E. Memorial Drive, Muncie, IN 47302, (765) 287-1256, Fax: (765) 289-4248 (www.modelaircraft.org).

The Northeast Electric Aircraft Technology (NEAT) Fair
It is one of the largest gatherings of electric airplane enthusiasts and suppliers in North America. (www.neatfair.org).

CHAPTER 13
Sources of Supplies

A&J Hobbies: www.ajhobby.com

Ace Sim RC: www.acesim.com/rc

AeroMicro: www.aeromicro.com

Aero-Model, Inc.: www.aero-model.com

Aerospace Composite Products:
   www.acp-composites.com

Aero Sport: www.aerosport.org

Airborne Models: www.airborne-models.com

Airtronics: www.airtronics.net

AMD Hobby: www.amdhobby.com

APC Propellers: www.apcprop.com

Apogee Batteries: (see PFM Distribution)

Art's Hobby: www.arts-hobby.com

Astro Flight Inc.: www.astroflight.com

Avia Sport Composites:
www.aviasport.net/links.htm

Aviat Aircraft: www.aviataircraft.com

AXI Motors: (see Hobby-Lobby)

Bambula Props: (see RC Showcase)

Batteries America: www.batteriesamerica.com

Berg Receivers: (see RC Direct)

Best RC Toys: www.best-rc-toys.com

BMJR Model Products: www.bmjrmodels.com

Bob Selman Designs: www.bsdmicrorc.com

Bob Smith Industries: www.bsiadhesives.com

BMV: www.bvmjets.com

Bob's Little Airplane Company: www.blac.net

Byron Originals: www.byronfuels.com

C. B. Associates/Tatone, Inc.:
   www.leisure-time.com/cba.htm

Cactus Aviation: www.cactusaviation.com

Carl Goldberg Products:
   www.carlgoldbergproducts.com

Castle Creations: www.castlecreations.com

Cedar Hobbies: www.cedarhobbies.com

Central Hobbies: www.centralhobbies.com

Century Helicopter Products:
   www.centuryheli.com

Cermark: www.cermark.com

Chief Aircraft Inc.: www.chiefaircraft.com

Cirrus: www.hobbypeople.net

Clancy Aviation: www.clancyaviation.com

Coverite: www.coverite.com

Curtek Systems: www.curtek.com

Dave Brown Products: www.dbproducts.com

Dave Patrick Models: www.davepatrickmodels.com

Dave's Aircraft Works: www.davesaircraftworks.com

DJ Aerotech: www.djaerotech.com

Du-Bro: www.dubro.com

Duralite Batteries: www.duralitebatteries.com

DuraTrax: www.duratrax.com

Dynamics Unlimited: www.slowfly.com

Dymond Modelsports: www.rc-dymond.com

Dynamics Unlimited: www.slowfly.com

Dynaflite: www.dynaflite.com

E Cubed R/C: www.azarr.com

Eagle Hobbies: www.eaglehobbies.com

Eagle Tree Systems: www.eagletreesystems.com

eDogFight.com: www.edogfight.com

E-Flite: (see Horizon Hobby Distributors)

ElectriCalc: www.slkelectronics.com/ecalc/

Electrifly by Great Planes: www.electrifly.com

Electronic Model Systems/JOMAR Products:
   www.emsjomar.com

Esprit Model: www.espritmodel.com

Estes-Cox Corporation: www.coxmodels.com

Extreme Flight RC: www.extremeflightrc.com
Flyzone by Hobbico: www.hobbico.com
FMA Direct: www.fmadirect.com
Frank Tiano Enterprises: www.franktiano.com
Futaba: www.futaba-rc.com
Gamma Star Models: www.gammastarmodels.com
Gator R/C: www.gatorrc.com
GiantScalePlanes: www.giantscaleplanes.com
Global Hobby Distributors: www.globalhobby.com
Great Planes Model Manufacturing:
    www.greatplanes.com
GWS: www.gws.com.tw/english/english.htm
Hacker Brushless Motors:
    www.hackerbrushless.com/airplanes.shtml
HalAir: www.halair.com
Hangar 9: (see Horizon Hobby Distributors)
HE-CELL: www.edogfight.com
Himaxx Motors: (see Maxx Products International)
Hitec RCD U.S.A., Inc.: www.hitecrcd.com
Hobbico: www.hobbico.com
Hobby E-store: www.hobby-estore.com
Hobby Hangar: www.hobbyhangar.com
Hobby Lobby International, Inc.:
    www.hobby-lobby.com
HobbyZone: www.hobbyzonesports.com
Horizon Hobby Distributors: www.horizonhobby.com
Hostetler's Plans: www.aero-sports.com/whplans
H. P. Pilots: www.hppilots.com
Ikarus U.S.A.: www.ikarus-usa.com
Indoor Model Supply:
    www.indoormodelsupply.com
Interactive Toy Concepts: www.interactivetoy.com
Jeti Motor Controls: (see Hobby-Lobby)

JR: www.jrradios.com
Just Go Fly: www.justgofly.com
Kangke Industrial USA Inc.: www.kangkeusa.com
Kondor Models: www.kmp.ca
Kyosho: www.kyosho.com
Landing Products: www.apcprop.com
Lanier RC: www.lanierrc.com
Lexors: (see Ikarus)
Lite Machines: www.litemachines.com
Litespan Covering by Hobby-Lobby:
    www.hobby-lobby.com/litespan.htm
Master Airscrew: (see Windsor Propeller Company)
Matney Models: www.matneymodels.com/
MaxCim Motors, Inc.: www.maxcim.com
Maxx Products International: www.maxxprod.com
MEC (Model Electronics Corporation):
    www.modelelectronicscorp.com
Mega Motor USA: www.megamotorusa.com
Megatech International: www.megatech.com
Microscale Industries: www.microscale.com
Mikado (see Aero-Model)
Mike's Hobby Tools: www.mikeshobbytools.com
Mikro Designs: www.mikrodesigns.com
Model Rectifier Corporation (MRC):
    www.modelrec.com
Model Motors: (see Hobby-Lobby)
Modelair-Tech: www.modelairtech.com
Modellbau USA: www.modellbau-usa.com
MotoCalc 7: www.motocalc.com
Mountain Models: www.mountainmodels.com
MP Jet: (see Hobby-Lobby)
MTM (Mike's Tiny Models) International:
    www.mtm-int.com

Nelson Hobby Specialties: www.nelsonhobby.com
Nelson Lite Film: (See Nelson Hobby Specialties)
Northeast Sailplane Products:
  www.nesail.com
Norvel: www.norvel.com
Ornithopter Zone: www.ornithopter.org/store
PK Industries: www.pkindustries.net
ParkZone: (see Horizon Hobby Distributors)
Peak Electronics: www.siriuselectronics.com
Peck-Polymers: www.peck-polymers.com
Penn Valley Hobby Center:
  www.pennvalleyhobbycenter.com
PFM Distribution: www.pfmdistribution.com
Plantraco: www.plantraco.com
Polk's Hobbies: www.polkshobby.com
Potensky: (see Hobby-Lobby)
Powermaster Hobby Products:
  www.powermasterfuels.com
Radical RC: www.radicalrc.com
Ram Radio Controlled Models:
  www.ramrcandramtrack.com
Razor Motors: www.razormotors.com
RC Direct: www.rc-direct.com
RC Hobby Center: www.rchobbycenter.com
RC Showcase: www.rcshowcase.com
RC Universe: www.rcuniverse.com.
RCAT Systems: www.rcatsystems.com
ReadyToFlyFun: readytoflyfun.com
RealFlight distributed by Great Planes Model
Distributors: www.realflight.com
RnR Products: www.rnrproducts.com
Robart Mfg.: www.robart.com
RN Models (see Peck-Polymus)
RT Models: www.rtmodels.com
SIG Manufacturing: www.sigmfg.com

Sky Hooks & Rigging: www.microrc.com
Slimline: www.slimlineproducts.com
SR Batteries: www.srbatteries.com
Startek International: www.startek.tv
Stevens AeroModel: www.stevensaero.com
Sullivan Products: www.sullivanproducts.com
SuperFly R/C: www.superflyrc.com
Tejera Microsystems Engineering: www.tmenet.com
Testor Corporation: www.testors.com
Thunder Power Batteries:
  www.thunderpower-batteries.com
Thunder Tiger: www.thundertiger.com
TnT Landing Gear Products:
  www.tntlandinggear.com
Todd's Models: www.toddsmodels.com
Top Flight Monokote: www.monokote.com
Tower Hobbies: www.towerhobbies.com
Trinity Products, Inc.: www.teamtrinity.com
Tru-Turn: www.tru-turn.com
Vel-Tye: www.veltye.com
Vintage R/C Society: www.vintagercsociety.org
W. S. Deans: www.wsdeans.com
Watt Age: www.watt-age.globalhobby.com
WES-Technik: www.wes-technik.de
West Mountain Radio:
www.westmountainradio.com
Wild R/C, Inc.: www.wildrc.com
Windrider R.S.B. Aviation Co., LTD.:
  www.windrider.com.hk
Windsor Propeller Company:
www.masterairscrew.com
Wing Warrior: www.wingwarrior.com
Wright Brothers R/C: www.wrightbrothersrc.com
Zinger Propeller: www.zingerpropeller.com
Z-Planes: www.zplanes.com

CHAPTER 14
Glossary

Ailerons: The control surfaces at the rear of the wing that are moved to allow the aircraft to bank or roll.

Airfoil: Any wing, rudder, elevator, stabilizer, propeller, and—on some aircraft—the fuselage that is designed to create a force or energy perpendicular to the air that is being forced around it.

Almost Ready to Fly (ARF): Aircraft models that have the major components—such as wings and fuselage—assembled but may require 1 to 5 hours of assembly time.

ARF: See almost ready to fly

Axial roll: When the aircraft rolls or rotates along the axis of the fuselage. In reality, few aircraft actually roll along the exact center. They rotate along the line of flight in a barrel roll.

Bank: When an aircraft leans to one side or the other during flight. Most real and model aircraft are designed to bank automatically when the rudder is set for a right or left turn.

Barrel roll: When an airplane rolls from conventional to inverted flight, it rotates on an axis that is its line of flight. In aerobatic competition, the barrel roll may sometimes be accomplished with aircraft performing a tight arc with the axis perhaps a few inches above the canopy.

Battery capacity: The measure of how long the battery will function at maximum current draw. Battery capacity is usually measured in mAh. A 720-mAh battery has potentially 720 milliamps. In reality, the battery will have something less than its rated capacity.

Built up: See stick models

CA: See cyanoacrylate adhesive

Channels: See frequency channels

Cyanoacrylate Adhesive (CA): The best-known brand is Super Glue, but there are special formulas for modelers, including CA that will not melt foam as it cures.

Delta wing: An aircraft design where the fuselage and wing are one piece with a triangular shape when viewed from the top. The term stems from the shape of the Greek letter delta.

Electronic speed control (ESC): The solid-state electronic device that transmits the radio control signals from the receiver to the motor to increase or decrease the motor's speed.

Elevator: The movable control surfaces at the rear of the horizontal stabilizer. The elevator is commonly used to change the aircraft's flight from level to climb or dive attitudes.

ESC: See electronic speed control

Flare: The term used for the control changes needed for an airplane's final touch down on landing.

Flat turn: A turn accomplished with the aircraft's wings perfectly parallel to the horizon. Since most aircraft (models or full-size) have built-in banking, the ailerons (and sometimes the elevator) must be moved to maintain a flat turn.

Flutter: When the rudder, elevator, or ailerons vibrate because there is too much slop in the control rod connections.

Frequency channels: The dedicated radio-transmitted commands from the radio control transmitter to the receiver. Each channel will transmit only commands on that specific frequency. Each control on the aircraft requires a separate channel. Most model airplanes have at least three: one for speed control through the ESC, one for the rudder control servo, and one for the elevator control servo.

Ground speed: How fast the aircraft is actually moving across the earth. It is measured by adding the aircraft's air speed to the speed of the wind. With a head wind, the aircraft may be flying much faster through the air but not making the same progress on the ground.

Horizontal stabilizer: The small wing at the extreme rear of most aircraft.

Knife-edge flight: The aerobatic model flies on its side with one wingtip pointed at the ground while the other points straight into the air. All lift is provided by the fuselage's side area. Strong top rudder control (the rudder is deflected away from the ground) is normally required to maintain level knife-edge flight.

Li-Poly batteries: See lithium-polymer batteries

Lithium-polymer batteries (Li-Poly): Currently, the lightest, most powerful, and expensive batteries available to power electric motors in model aircraft.

Loop: An aerobatic maneuver where the aircraft makes a 360-degree curve vertical to the ground.
National Model Aviation Championships (NATS): They are held each year in Muncie, Indiana, and are sponsored by the Academy of Model Aeronautics (AMA). This is the largest event in America for flying model aircraft and several thousand participants compete. The NATS are primarily for fuel-powered models. There are also competitive and demonstration events for electric-powered aircraft.

Pattern: The extreme form of aerobatic competition where the pilots perform specific, precise aerobatic maneuvers and five points are taken off for any deviation from perfect circles or shaky movements of the aircraft. These events are managed by the National Society of Radio Controlled Aerobatics (NSRCA).

Pitch: One of the three control directions (yaw, pitch, and roll) for an airplane. It is when an aircraft tilts, end-to-end, to lower the nose or tail during flight. With some aircraft, moving the rudder automatically induces a slight nose-down pitch. The term is also applied to propellers or rotors to describe how far the propeller will move the aircraft.

Profile: A model that is cut from sheets of foam or balsa and has a simple flat fuselage, rudder, stabilizer, and wings. Some profile models may have airfoil-shaped wings to provide better aerobatic performance.

Roll: One of the three control directions (yaw, pitch, and roll) for an airplane. It is a flying or aerobatic maneuver where the aircraft is pivoted along the axis of fuselage, usually to change from normal to inverted flight.

Scale: Scale is the proportion of the model compared with the size of the real aircraft. For example, if a model is 1/32 scale, it will be 1/32nd the size of the real aircraft. If the real aircraft had a 30-foot (360-inch) wingspan, the 1/32 scale model would have an 11.25-inch (360 ÷ 32 = 11.25) wingspan. Few of the ready-to-fly or ARF model aircraft are labeled a specific scale. Some of the kits have a designated scale.

Stall: When the aircraft is flying too slowly to provide enough lift to keep the aircraft in the air. If the stall is not caught and/or corrected, the aircraft will fall to the earth.

Stick models: The traditional method of building an inner structure from sheet balsa bulkheads and balsa strip spars. These aircraft are often called stick models because the kit box contains a large pile of balsa sticks.

Throttle notches: The control levers or joystick on most radio controlled transmitters have small notches that are designed to provide a tactile feedback so you know how far you're moving the stick without needing to look down at the transmitter.

Touch and go: A maneuver used to help train pilots of real and model aircraft to land the aircraft. The aircraft is maneuvered into landing position and all the landing techniques are used until the aircraft's wheels touch down. Instead of backing off on the throttle, the throttle is pushed forward so the aircraft can take off again.

Trim levers: Most transmitters have small levers near the control sticks that are used to make fine adjustments of the control surfaces that will remain in effect. Some transmitters allow you to program these adjustments so you can reuse them the next time you fly that particular aircraft.

X-Port Enabled: It is the term HobbyZone uses for the command option for the connection to the optional Sonic Combat Unit that signals shots and hits for combat flying.

Yaw: One of the three control directions (yaw, pitch, and roll) for an airplane. Yaw control moves the fuselage left or right.

Index

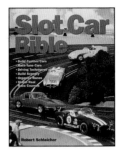
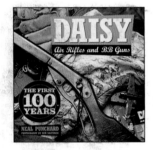